back to BASICS

PAT YAMIN

QUILT
TEMPLATES
& PATTERNS
EXPLAINED

American Quilter's Society
P. O. Box 3290 • Paducah, KY 42002-3290
www.AQSquilt.com

Located in Paducah, Kentucky, the American Quilter's Society (AQS) is dedicated to promoting the accomplishments of today's quilters. Through its publications and events, AQS strives to honor today's quiltmakers and their work and to inspire future creativity and innovation in quiltmaking.

EDITOR: HELEN SQUIRE
GRAPHIC DESIGN: ELAINE WILSON
COVER DESIGN: MICHAEL BUCKINGHAM
PHOTOGRAPHY: CHARLES R. LYNCH

Library of Congress Cataloging-in-Publication Data
Yamin, Pat
    Back to Basics: quilt templates and patterns explained / by Pat
Yamin
        p. cm.
        ISBN 1-57432-824-7
1.   Patchwork--Patterns. 2.   Quilting--Patterns.   I. Title.

TT835.Y34 2003
    746.46--dc21

                                2003014654

Additional copies of this book may be ordered from the American Quilter's Society, PO Box 3290, Paducah, KY 42002-3290; 800-626-5420 (orders only please); or online at www.AQSquilt.com. For all other inquiries, call 270-898-7903.

Copyright © 2003, Pat Yamin

dedication

I would like to dedicate this book to the students who have taken my classes, and to all of my family and friends who encouraged me in this project.

To my parents, who are no longer with me, thank you for teaching me to constantly strive to do my very best, and to always be there for the other guy.

Above all, I want to thank my husband, Steve, and my son, Jared, for your love and continuous support.

acknowledgments

I would like to sincerely thank the following people and companies for making this book a reality: Meredith Schroeder, at the *American Quilter's Society,* for giving me the opportunity to write this book, and Helen Squire for helping me through the editing process. To the ladies who made the quilts in the book, and to the following people I am especially grateful: Marge Ahearn, Nancy Cerza, Shirley Greenhoe, Judy Hahner, Kathy Jones, Nancy Stirtz, and Jackie Wolff.

Also to the companies who have provided the products and fabrics I recommend, I appreciate your help in making this book complete; Benartex Inc., Clover Needlecraft Inc., Free Spirit, Marcus Brothers, Prym Dritz Corp., Quilts and Other Comforts, Rowenta, and The Colonial Needle Co.

Helen and Elaine, thanks from the bottom of my heart...

contents

introduction

I began collecting old quilt blocks and quilt tops in the late 1960s at flea markets in the Northeast. The old fabric that was used to make these simple patterns peaked my interest to learn more about the history of old blocks and quilts. Sometimes men's dress shirts, women's dresses and even aprons were used to piece these blocks together. Many were often handstitched, with coarse double thread. I liked them because each one was unique in its own way. I nicknamed the blocks "orphans," as they never made it into a quilt. They were left for someone else to finish one day. All of these old blocks had interesting names such as Churn Dash, Monkey Wrench, Milky Way, Anvil and Spool, plus many others. I think many of these names came from everyday life in the 1800s. Many of the block pattern names were changed when a pattern was traded with another quilter, or when a quilter and her family moved to a new town, a pattern was given a name appropriate to the area. Some patterns such as Wild Goose Chase, Ducklings, Fox and Geese, Hen and Chickens, Corn and Beans, Handy Andy, and Shoo Fly are all names given to the same block! Being interested in history, the lives of our grandmothers led me to look for more blocks, more fabric, and to the study of old quilt patterns.

I own several of the old newspaper quilt patterns that appeared in *The Kansas City Star*, and *The Weekly Star Farmer* newspapers from 1928 to 1961. When the patterns were all compiled and published by the Central Oklahoma Quilter's Guild in the late 1980s, I gratefully purchased the complete pattern set. Many of these patterns were created and submitted to the newspapers by women who lived in the rural areas of Kansas, Missouri, Oklahoma, and Arkansas. The pattern names often reflected a glimpse of America and what was happening in our history at that time. I also referred to Barbara Brackman and her book *An Encyclopedia of Pieced Quilt Patterns* (American Quilter's Society, 1993). Both of these have been great resources for choosing the blocks for this book. I wanted to present a collection of patterns that would be easy for the beginner while offering more advanced blocks for the experienced quiltmaker.

The most common shapes of the old patterns are the square, half-square triangle, and quarter-square triangle. In the template section (pages 103–108) are the templates to create the blocks from six to twelve inches in size. All of the template shapes are offered in several sizes. There are over 175 blocks in this ready-to-use format, however, the design possibilities on blocks to sew are endless. I have researched thousands of quilt patterns and chosen blocks that can be made from the 18 templates offered. I think this will save you an enormous amount of time.

I would love to hear from you. Whether you decide just to make lots of blocks, or blocks into tops... send me a snapshot to share with my students. See the resource guide on page 109 for the CQWM address.

Happy quilting,

Pat Yamin

general instructions

QUILTING SUPPLIES

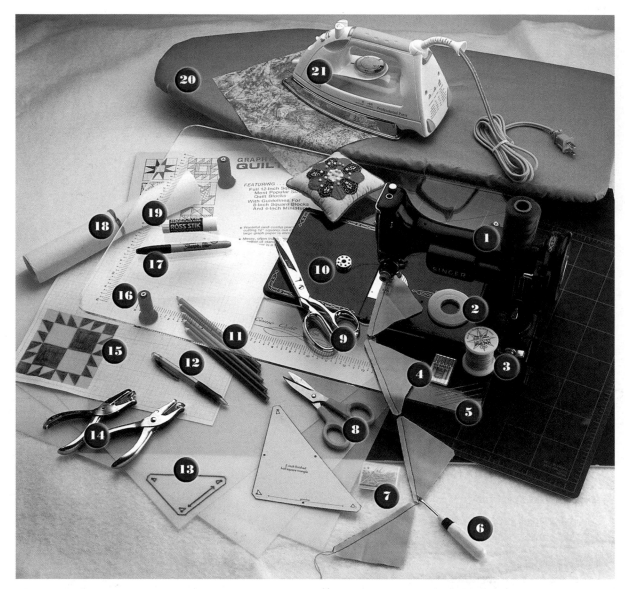

Basic Items

1. Sewing Machine
2. Masking Tapes: ¼" and
   2" Masking Tape (not shown)
3. Sewing Thread
4. Machine Needles
5. Needles:
   #10 Quilting Betweens
6. Seam Ripper
7. Straight Pins
8. Utility Scissors
9. Fabric Scissors
10. Extra Threaded Bobbins
11. Colored Pencils
12. Mechanical Pencil
13. Opaque Plastic
14. Hole Punch: ⅛" or ¼"
15. Graph Paper: ¼" grid
16. Acrylic Work Table
17. Indelible Pen – fine point
18. Rubber Bands
19. Glue Stick
20. Ironing Board
21. Steam Iron

back *to* BASICS ◆ Pat Yamin

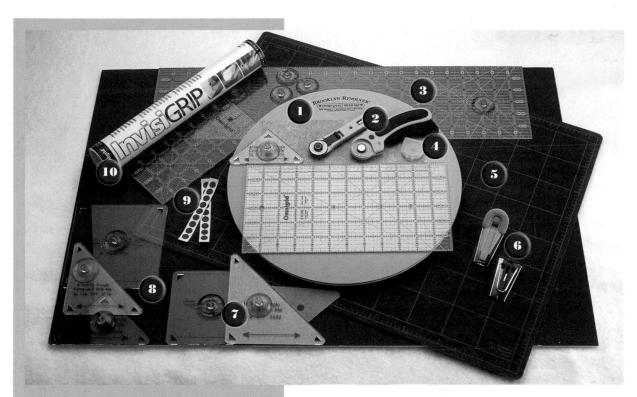

Time Saving Tools

1. Brooklyn Revolver™

2. Rotary Cutters

3. Acrylic Rulers:
4" x 8", 6" x 12", 6" x 24"

4. Extra Rotary Blades

5. Cutting Mat

6. Bias Tape Makers

7. Suction Cups

8. Acrylic Templates from
Come Quilt With Me™

9. Sandpaper Dots

10. InvisiGRIP™ Non-Slip Material

Quilting Necessities

1. Polyester or Cotton Batting

2. Quilting Hoop

3. Safety Pins

4. Thimbles

5. Threads: Basting and Quilting

6. Needles: #7 Long Darners,
#10 Quilting Betweens, not shown

SELECTING FABRICS

The best fabric for you to use in making your quilts is 100 percent cotton fabric. This is one area where you do not want to compromise. There is a sign at my local car dealership that says, "Quality is not expensive, it's Priceless." This is so true for all of us when we are choosing the fabric for our quilts. Buy the best that you can, because you want your quilt to last for generations. Less expensive cottons are usually loosely woven with a lesser thread count per inch, which sometimes causes them to stretch and distort the fabric piece. When you are buying your fabric, do not be afraid to select a yard or two of some wild or loud color. You will be surprised how this will make your imagination soar. Have some fun at the fabric store!

FABRIC PREPARATION

There are different views on the best way to prepare your fabric for your quilt. I believe you should wash and dry all of it before you cut. It is especially important that 100 percent cotton fabric be washed to allow for the shrinkage in the yardage for your project. You also want to wash out the chemicals used to treat the fabric.

Machine wash in warm water, place it in the dryer, and remove just before it is completely dry. This makes it easier to iron out all those wrinkles. If you think your material has lost "body" in the washing process, add spray starch or fabric sizing when you are ironing.

MAKING TEMPLATES

All of the pattern pieces used in making the blocks and quilts shown are given in actual size templates in the back of the book, pages 103–108.

When making templates, I prefer the corners to be double cut so you never have the "dog ears" on your pieces. Each piece matches up perfectly, taking the guesswork out of adjusting the pattern pieces. The templates are designed for machine or hand piecing.

For machine piecing Trace the template using a Sanford Sharpie® (a fine point marking pen with indelible ink). Lay the template plastic over the pattern piece and trace the outside line. The ¼" seam allowance is included.

For hand piecing Follow the same method, trace the design, and then use your ⅛" or ¼" hole punch to mark the ¼" at the corners, and maybe once along the seam allowance line.

It is important that all of the templates be cut out carefully. If they are not accurate, the pieces will not fit together properly!

Mark the size and the grain line on each template piece with the marking pen. It's usually a good idea to test one set of templates before you cut out all your pieces.

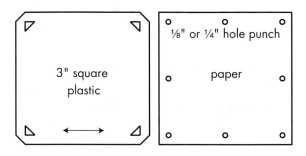

Templates made from plastic for machine piecing or paper for hand piecing

Making one sample block will show you that you have traced and cut out the pieces accurately. I use sandpaper dots on the back of the templates to prevent the template from sliding when I am cutting the fabric.

CUTTING TECHNIQUES
Rotary Cutting

You need to "square up" the fabric before the fabric is cut into strips. Fold the fabric in half lengthwise and half again. This will give you four layers to cut through. Lay the fabric on your cutting surface, keeping the folded edges turned toward your body. Using the long ruler as your guide, position the ruler so that you have a horizontal line on the fold of the fabric, and a vertical line straight (parallel) with the fabric grain (Diagram 1–1). Cut off the selvage from the fabric, usually a ½" piece imprinted with the company's name or colored dots.

Next, measure the height of the template and cut strips from the front of the fold that are ½" taller than your template height. This will allow for accuracy when you are cutting multiple layers of fabric. A strip is the basic unit that will be used to cut shapes.

Pay close attention to the grain lines of the fabric. Place the template on the straight edges of the fabric, parallel to the grain lines (Diagram 1–2).

A rotary cutter is fast because you can cut multiple layers at one time. It is also more accurate than using scissors since the fabric is flat and does not move. However, accuracy is more important than speed, so take your time if you are a beginner using this tool.

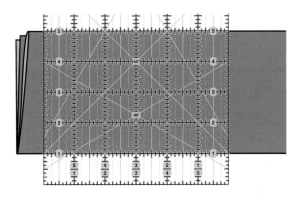

Diagram 1–1. Use the long ruler as your guide on the fold of the fabric.

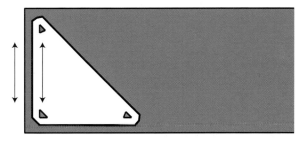

Diagram 1–2. Use the grain lines on the straight edge of the fabric.

Tip: I raise all of my tables to 42", which is my hip height. This makes cutting much easier and faster. Cut along each side of the square, rotating the cutting mat while still holding down the template. I recommend the Brooklyn Revolver™ rotating cutting mat. Because you can cut, rotate, and cut you never move the template or the fabric so you are guaranteed accurate cutting. After cutting one square, move the template along the fabric strip. Then cut another square the same as the first. Leave a space between cuts.

Caution: You should never use a cut line as your new edge. If you have slipped your error will be multiplied.

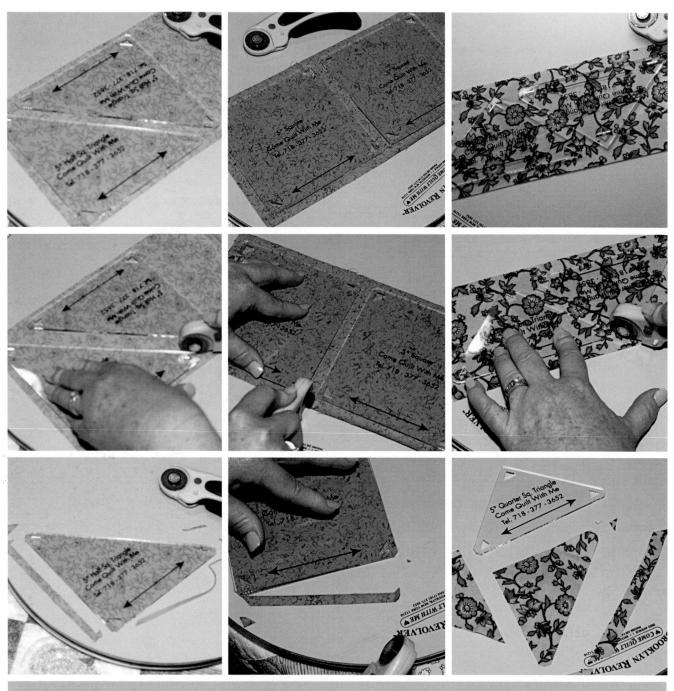

Cutting Half-Square Triangles

Cutting Squares

Cutting Quarter-Square Triangles

When cutting your pieces, lay your template on the strip with ¼" inch more of fabric on the top and bottom of the template height. Place your cutter about ¼" into the strip and cut backwards first; then cut almost to the edge of the piece, and lift up the cutter again. This time cut from the corner, back along the side of the template, and then off straight. This way you will never have wobbly ears at the end.

Take a strip of the cut fabric and lay it on your cutting mat. If you have several layers, position the fabric so you can see all four layers (Diagram 1-3). This prevents the fabric layers from shifting.

As an example, use the square template as your first attempt. Lay the template on the strip with extra fabric all around (Diagram 1–4).

Place the suction cup in the middle of the template. Use the suction cup as a finger grip to firmly hold the template in place while you cut the fabric. Place the blade of the rotary cutter flush against the side of the template, holding the cutter at a 45 degree angle with the fabric.

Always cut away from your body.

Hand Cutting

Lay the template on the wrong side of a single layer strip of fabric. Position it so that the straight edges of the template are on the straight edges of the fabric.

Keep the long sides of the triangles on the true bias by placing the short sides on the straight of fabric. Holding the template in place with your suction cup, trace around the template using the mechanical pencil. Continue moving the template across the length of the strip, tracing it on the fabric (Diagram 1-5). Remember not to share previous seam lines. Use a sharp pair of scissors to cut out your pieces, being careful not to lift up the fabric while cutting.

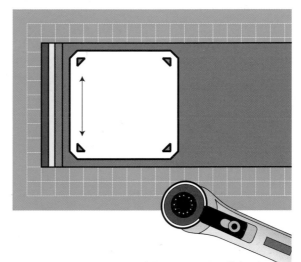

Diagram 1–3. Position fabric to view all the layers.

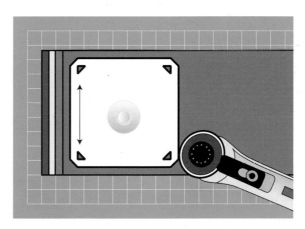

Diagram 1–4. The rotary cutter is placed at a 45° angle.

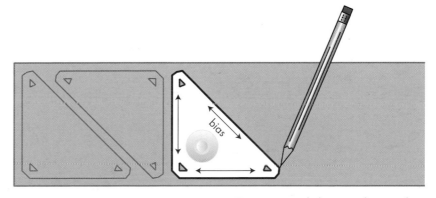

Diagram 1–5. Trace around the template with a mechanical or sharp pencil.

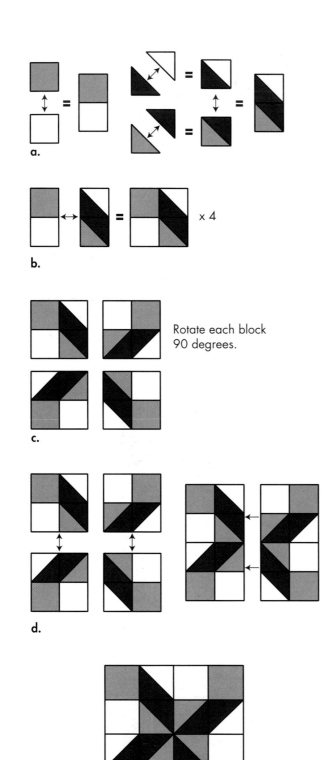

a.

b.

Rotate each block 90 degrees.

c.

d.

e.

Diagram 1–6. Piecing of a Four-Patch pattern, Clay's Choice block. Pattern on page 98.

STITCHING

The first step in piecing a quilt block is to study the block and break it down into units. Look for repeating patterns within the design and see how they build on each other to make the finished block. The individual units should be sewn together before you begin to piece the block. You will notice that some of the units are single pieces, while others may be a quarter section of the block (Diagram 1–6a to 1–6e).

When piecing by hand or machine, use pins to match up your seams. A pin carefully pushed through the fabric to match the ¼" seam allowances will ensure accuracy (Diagram 1-7, page 15).

HAND SEWING

Place two shapes together with right sides facing, and place a pin through both of the pieces at the ¼" mark at either end. Stitch with a single thread no longer than 18" long. To secure the stitch, begin at the ¼" seam line, take a stitch, and then backstitch without making a knot. Use a quilting betweens needle to sew the pieces with an even running stitch (Diagram 1–7). Try to keep the seam as straight as possible, sewing alongside of the pencil line. (If you sew through the pencil line, your thread will get "dirty.") Keep the thread taut enough so the edges do not stretch as you sew them. Backstitch at the end of the seam line. Press the pieces with the seams going to one side, toward the darker fabric.

MACHINE PIECING

The ¼" seam allowance was included when you cut your pieces. The presser foot on some sewing machines is marked for sewing the ¼" seam allowance. If yours is not, then measure ¼" from the needle hole toward the right side of your presser foot and place a piece of the ¼" masking tape on the plate.

A good straight stitch is all that is necessary to piece your quilt blocks. I prefer the stitch length to be 10 to 12 stitches per inch. Place two pieces of fabric right sides together, with the raw edges aligned. If you are working with pieces less than 4" long, I do not think it is necessary to pin when you are machine piecing. Begin and end stitching at the raw edges without backstitching.

To chain stitch a lot of small pieces, feed pairs of fabric under the pressure foot while taking a few stitches without any fabric under the needle between pairs (Diagram 1-8). This requires some practice, but once you start sewing in this manner, it saves a lot of time. Cut apart your "Christmas chain." Press the pieces with the seams going to one side.

JOINING THE BLOCKS

After you have pieced the blocks for your quilting project, lay them out on your table, or better yet, audition them vertically on a piece of flannel. It is always a good idea to arrange them a few different ways to see which position you really like. You may choose the traditional setting of blocks next to blocks, or you may want to have your blocks joined on point. For this method the blocks are joined sewing the rows together on a diagonal.

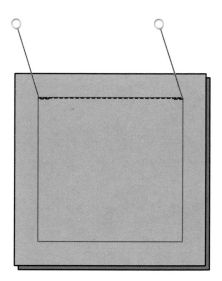

Diagram 1–7. For hand sewing no knots are needed. Backstitch at the start and at the end of the seam line. Leave seam allowances free for easier pressing.

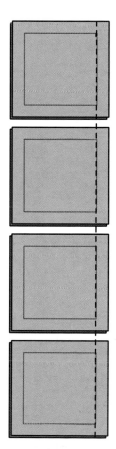

Diagram 1–8. For machine stitching, sew through the seam allowances. Begin and end stitching without backstitching. Chain stitch pieces together.

Sometimes when the diagonal method is used, a plain block (called a space block) is alternated with a pieced block. The decision to use space blocks means less pieced blocks will be needed.

Begin joining by pinning at each end of the block and then put a pin in the center of the block matching the center seams. It is usually a good idea to have one row of seams going to the right and the other going to the left. Using ¼" seam allowance, join all of the blocks together, working in rows.

SASHING AND BORDERS

A traditional quilt uses sashing pieced between the blocks as shown in Diagram 1–9. Traditionally the sashing width will vary from 2" to 4". Once all of your blocks are completed, cut your sashing into short strips, the same width as one side of your block. Again, the width of the sashing is up to you. Once you have sewn the columns, piece them together with long strips of sashing that extend the length and width of the quilt. A second contrasting border can be added around the quilt if desired. Carefully press the entire quilt top.

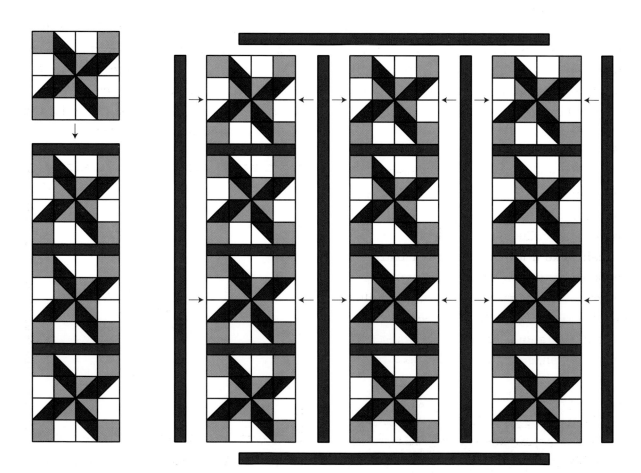

Diagram 1–9. Assembling and piecing the quilt top with sashing strips

BACKING FABRIC

This is the really fun part of making the quilt because you can go wild and make your own yardage from all of the scraps that were left from the top. Or you may want to be conservative and have a floral or a muted tone-on-tone as your backing. Whatever you choose, buy the same quality fabric for the back as the top.

Never use a sheet or designer fabric, since both have a higher thread count and it's very hard to quilt through. (I have tried it!) Remove the selvages from both sides of the fabric. You want to measure at least 4" more all around the sides of your quilt. It's okay to have either a vertical or horizontal seam. On the backing seams I use a ½" seam allowance and sew down the seam twice. Since this is a very long seam, I want to be sure the seam doesn't open in the quilting process. Press the backing seams open to lay flat.

BATTING

There are numerous types of battings in the quilt market today. You need to decide before you buy the batting how your quilt is going to be quilted. For hand quilting projects I really like a low loft polyester batting. It makes the quilting easier and you will be more successful with making small quilting stitches. If you plan to machine quilt, I still recommend a low loft batting but you can buy this in cotton, polyester, or even wool.

Tip: You should iron the quilt top before basting and quilting. Also, cut off the loose threads from the front and back and check for any open seams.

QUILT BASTING

This is when you invite all of those good quilting friends over for a dinner. Place the backing and batting on a large clean surface. A floor is usually a good choice. Spread the backing out wrong side up and smooth out any wrinkles. I recommend using two inch masking tape to tape the backing down in six inch intervals to keep it from moving. Spread the batting over the backing and smooth out any wrinkles. Do this part ahead of time as sometimes the batting needs to be smoothed over several times. Carefully place the top face up over the backing and batting. Beginning in the center, baste the three layers together with either safety pins or thread.

Baste the quilt 4" apart (the width of your palm) from the center of the quilt out to the edge in a radiating pattern. Taking the time to baste your quilt securely will make quilting it a lot easier (Diagram 1-10 and Diagram 1-11, shown on page 18).

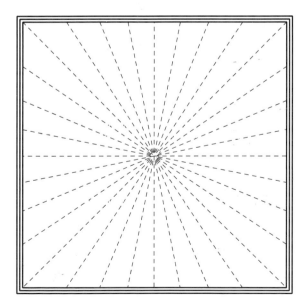

Diagram 1–10. Radiate basting from the center. Use the width of your palm as a guide.

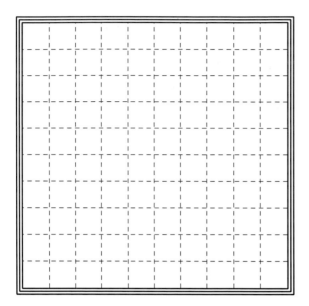

Diagram 1-11. Grid baste rows 4"–6" apart. Secure all three layers.

Detail of antique quilt used on the cover showing hand quilting

HAND QUILTING

I really love to hand quilt, and consider it to be the "bonus" of the quilt project. However, with a busy schedule I sometimes choose to send my quilts out to be machine quilted.

How much hand quilting you will need to do depends on the batting you choose. Generally, cotton batting will require more quilting than polyester batting.

To begin quilting, cut a length of thread no longer than 18". Make a very small knot about ½" from the end of the thread. Take one or two small quilting stitches and give the thread a quick tug. This will pop the thread into the backing and batting. Continue to make short even running stitches through all of the layers. The stitches should be evenly spaced with the spaces between stitches about the same length as the stitches themselves.

The number of stitches per inch is not as important as the consistency of the stitch. You will get better with practice, and get your own stitching rhythm going.

To end the thread, take one very small backstitch. Push the point of the needle and thread through the backstitch and under the quilt top. Bring up your needle an inch away from where you made the backstitch. Carefully cut off the remaining thread.

Tip: When thread basting, use a 36" length color-contrasting thread, double strand, and knotted at the end. I like John James #7 Long Darners. They are very long and thin and the heat of your hand warms the needle to create a slight bend.

MACHINE QUILTING

Use cotton thread (size 50) or cotton-covered polyester to thread your machine and your bobbin. If you want stitches to be invisible on your quilt top, use cotton thread in the bobbin and a monofilament nylon thread for top stitches.

Stitches should be even on the top and bottom of the quilt. It may be necessary to adjust the top and/or bobbin tensions to obtain an even stitch. Do not attempt to machine quilt your first project without practicing first. Prepare a small practice quilt sandwich using backing, batting, and fabric. Machine stitch on this piece until you feel comfortable with the process.

The simplest method for machine quilting is to stitch-in-the-ditch around each shape and on both sides of the sashing (Diagram 1–12). For a grid effect, stitch with straight lines, working from the center of the quilt to one side; turn and then stitch to the opposite side. Complete all horizontal lines, and then stitch all vertical lines.

Two other machine techniques are the "walking foot" method and "free-motion" quilting. A walking foot enables the quilt sandwich to feed evenly through the machine without the layers shifting.

For free-motion quilting, it is necessary to use an open foot such as an embroidery or darning foot. However, you will need to drop the feed dogs. If you cannot drop the feed dogs, cover them with an index card. You control the length of the stitch as you feed the quilt sandwich through the machine

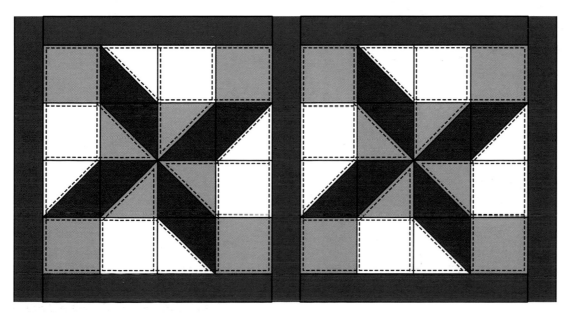

Diagram 1–12. On the side of the seam without seam allowance, stitch-in-the-ditch. Outline quilt around the shape of the design.

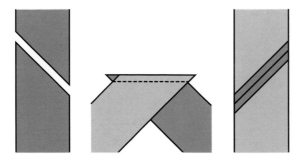

Diagram 1–13. Cut strip ends with 45° angle and sew together as shown. Open and press seams.

Diagram 1–14. Single layer binding

Diagram 1–15. Double layer binding

Diagram 1–16. Blind stitch the binding to the back of the quilt.

BINDING

Finish your quilt by trimming off the excess batting and backing. Carefully remove the safety pins or pull out the basting stitches. To make your own binding, cut 2" widths of fabric either on the bias or straight grain of the fabric. End each strip by cutting on a 45 degree angle and sew all of the strips together. You will need enough binding to go around the entire quilt. Measure your width and length; multiply by two and add eight extra inches for safety (Diagram 1-13).

To make single layer binding: Iron the binding in half so it is now 1" wide. Open the binding and match up one raw edge of the binding with the quilt top, right sides facing each other. Stitch the binding to the quilt top ¼" from the edge (Diagram 1-14). Fold the binding to the back of the quilt and turn under the edge ¼". Using a blind stitch, sew the binding to the back of your quilt.

To make a double layer binding: Prepare the binding strips in the same manner as above, cutting the strips 2½" wide. Fold the binding in half wrong sides together. Match up the raw edges of the binding to the raw edges of your quilt. Stitch a ¼" seam allowance attaching the two layers of binding to the top of the quilt edge (Diagram 1–15). Then fold over the binding and blind stitch to the back of the quilt (Diagram 1–16).

Tip: Use a straight pin to anchor Clover™ Needlecraft Inc. bias tape maker to ironing board cover. This will free up both hands to feed and iron the fabric for bias binding.

pattern section

this is a how-to manual for cutting and assembling popular, old-time patchwork patterns using today's accurate templates and rotary cutting techniques.

All 175 block patterns are made from only three basic shapes: the square, the half-square triangle, and the quarter-square triangle. Choose your own colors and fabrics, but keep in mind the tonal values – light, medium, and dark. That's what makes each block different and unique.

Look for the scrap fabric icon. ⓢ It symbolizes patterns that traditionally used small pieces from the scrap bag to create the design.

The patterns are divided by recommended skill levels: easy, intermediate, and advanced, but these groups overlap. I've included Nine-Patch, repetitive Four-Patch, and favorite Five-Patch throughout.

In other words, this book has something for everyone!

Cutting amounts are provided for individual blocks. Mix and match the template shapes and sizes to the pattern illustration. For quilts, multiply the number of cut pieces by how many blocks you will need.

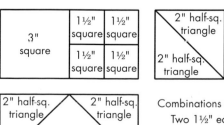

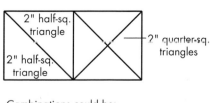

Combinations could be:
Two 1½" equal 3"
Two 2" equal 4"
Two 2½" equal 5" and so on...

Examples of the breakdown of the pattern pieces for the blocks

easy patterns

intermediate patterns

advanced patterns

to the housewife of the Midwest, newspapers were one of their greatest sources for quilt patterns. The weekly quilt pattern was treasured, carefully clipped, and saved. *The Kansas City Star* published weekly quilt patterns from 1928 to 1961. Pattern series from *The Weekly Star Farmer* and *The Star* also influenced quilting at the time. Over one thousand patterns where published! These patterns continue to play an important part in preserving the art, history, and design of quiltmaking today.

Quilters traded and shared quilt patterns with family and friends. They started sending their own quilt block designs to the newspaper. Four hundred and fifty quilt patterns from contributors were published. Most listed the quilter's name – primarily ladies, with a few men, young girls, and boys. If a design was accepted for publication (accompanied by a completed fabric block) the contributor was paid $1.50.

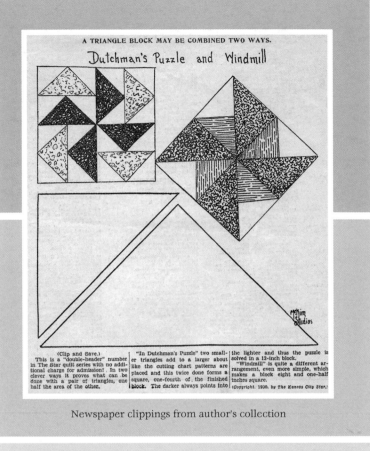

Newspaper clippings from author's collection

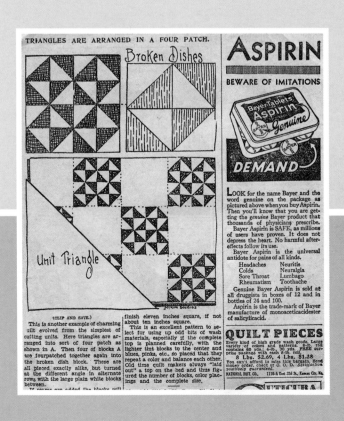

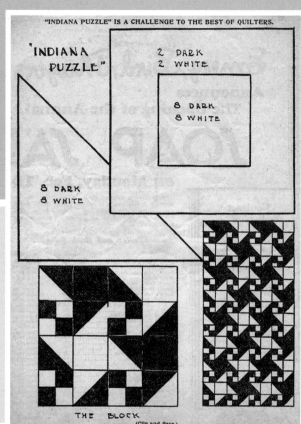

"INDIANA PUZZLE" IS A CHALLENGE TO THE BEST OF QUILTERS.

"INDIANA PUZZLE"

2 DARK
2 WHITE

8 DARK
8 WHITE

8 DARK
8 WHITE

THE BLOCK
(Clip and Save.)

This intricate pattern comes from Indiana. It is remarkably effective, considering the simplicity of the patches, and makes a very striking quilt pieced in dark blue and white. The block, when finished, is sixteen inches square. This pattern will arouse the interest of quilt makers who get their keenest enjoyment out of piecing difficult patterns, as it is considered by many to be more difficult to put together than "The Old Maid's Puzzle." In piecing it, sew patches together in rows and join rows. No seams are allowed.
(Copyright, 1930, by The Kansas City Star.)

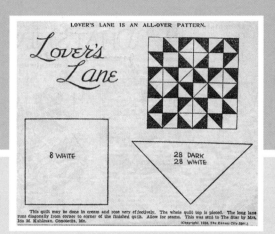

LOVER'S LANE IS AN ALL-OVER PATTERN.

Lover's Lane

8 WHITE

28 DARK
28 WHITE

This quilt may be done in cream and rose very effectively. The whole quilt top is pieced. The long lane runs diagonally from corner to corner of the finished quilt. Allow for seams. This was sent to The Star by Mrs. Ida M. Kuhlman, Concordia, Mo.
(Copyright, 1936, The Kansas City Star.)

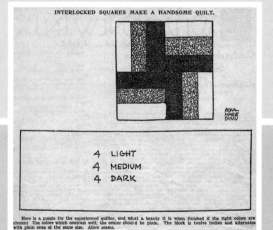

INTERLOCKED SQUARES MAKE A HANDSOME QUILT.

EDNA MARIE DUNN

4 LIGHT
4 MEDIUM
4 DARK

Here is a puzzle for the experienced quilter, and what a beauty it is when finished if the right colors are chosen! Use colors which contrast well; the center should be plain. The block is twelve inches and alternates with plain ones of the same size. Allow seams.
(Copyright, The Kansas City Star, 1932.)

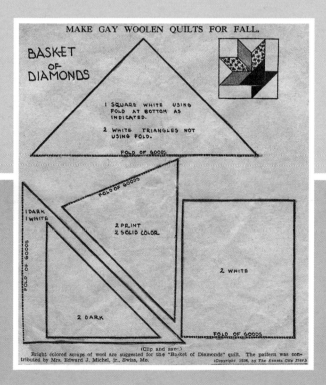

MAKE GAY WOOLEN QUILTS FOR FALL.

BASKET OF DIAMONDS

1 SQUARE WHITE USING FOLD AT BOTTOM AS INDICATED.

2 WHITE TRIANGLES NOT USING FOLD.

FOLD OF GOODS

FOLD OF GOODS

1 DARK
1 WHITE

FOLD OF GOODS

2 PRINT
2 SOLID COLOR

2 WHITE

2 DARK

FOLD OF GOODS

(Clip and save.)
Bright colored scraps of wool are suggested for the "Basket of Diamonds" quilt. The pattern was contributed by Mrs. Edward J. Michel, Jr., Swiss, Mo.
(Copyright, 1936, by The Kansas City Star.)

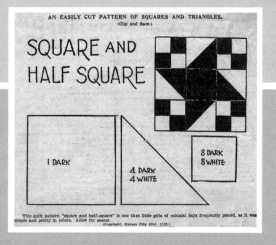

AN EASILY CUT PATTERN OF SQUARES AND TRIANGLES.
(Clip and Save.)

SQUARE AND HALF SQUARE

1 DARK

4 DARK
4 WHITE

8 DARK
8 WHITE

This quilt pattern "square and half-square" is one that little girls of colonial days frequently pieced, as it was simple and pretty in colors. Allow for seams.
(Copyright, Kansas City Star, 1933.)

Newspaper clippings from author's collection

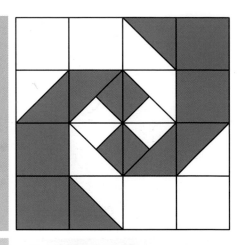

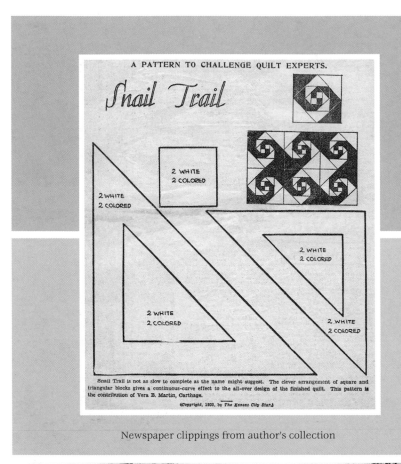

Snail Trail

block sizes 6", 8", 10", 12"

8 – lg. squares
   4 light, & 4 dark
12 – lg. half-sq. triangles
   6 light, & 6 dark
8 – sm. quarter-sq. triangles
   4 light, & 4 dark

SNAIL'S TRAIL

Gayle Brockway Noyes
Post Falls, ID

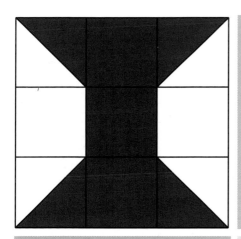

Spool

block sizes 6", 9", 12"

5 – lg. squares
   2 light, & 3 dark

8 – lg. half-sq. triangles
   4 light, & 4 dark

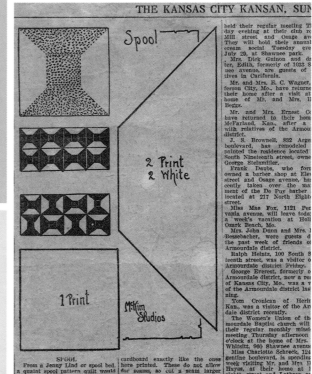

SPOOL QUILT
Marge Geary
Williston Park, NY

f quilt designers Ruby McKim, Rose Kessinger, and Nancy Cabot were the legends of the last century, then the historians and researchers were the heroes.

Barbara Brackman, Carrie Hall, Yvonne M. Khin, and Shirley Liby are among those who have dedicated their time and talents to preserving the patterns of the past. (See Bibliography, pg. 109).

From newspaper articles to entire encyclopedias on the subject, quilt pattern collections have come a long way! Today's quilters can benefit from the history and research done yesterday while making their quilts for tomorrow.

Quilt block design by Nancy Cabot

Baton Rouge Square

block size 10"

17 – sm. squares
    8 light, 5 medium & 4 dark
16 – sm. half-sq. triangles
    8 light, & 8 dark

BATON ROUGE SQUARE

Rita Rehm
Hebron, CT

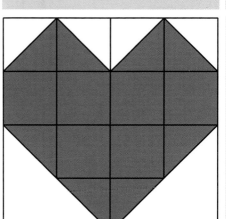

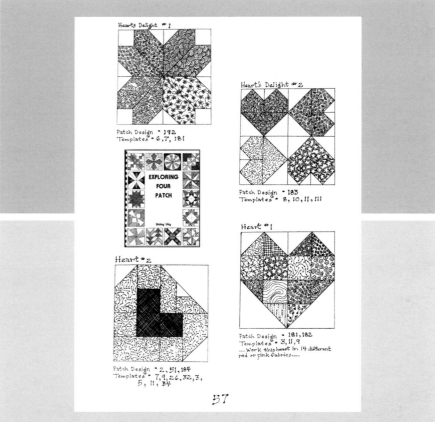

From Shirley Liby's book *Exploring Four Patch* ©1988 Shirley Liby

Heart

block sizes 6", 8", 10"

- 2 – lg. half-sq. triangles
  light
- 6 – med. squares, dark
- 12 – med. half-sq. triangles
  4 light, & 8 dark

HEART QUILT
Laura Lipski
Lindenhurst, NY

easy

CARMEN'S BLOCK

Rosalba Kite
Kutztown, PA

before you begin sewing, make sure to have at least three full bobbins. I can't tell you how many times I continued to sew and then realized my bobbin was empty and the pieces were all laying on the floor!

cut your border fabric first. Then measure the height of the templates to be used and cut the fabric into strips. I always give an extra ½" to the template height. This way the template has an extra ¼" on the top and bottom. When cutting several layers, the template will always be accurate.

Carmen's Block
block sizes 6", 8", 10"

2 – lg. squares, dark
8 – sm. squares
    4 light & 4 medium

Squares Upon Squares

block sizes 6", 8", 10"

1 – lg. square, dark
12 – sm. squares
　　3 light, 6 medium & 3 dark

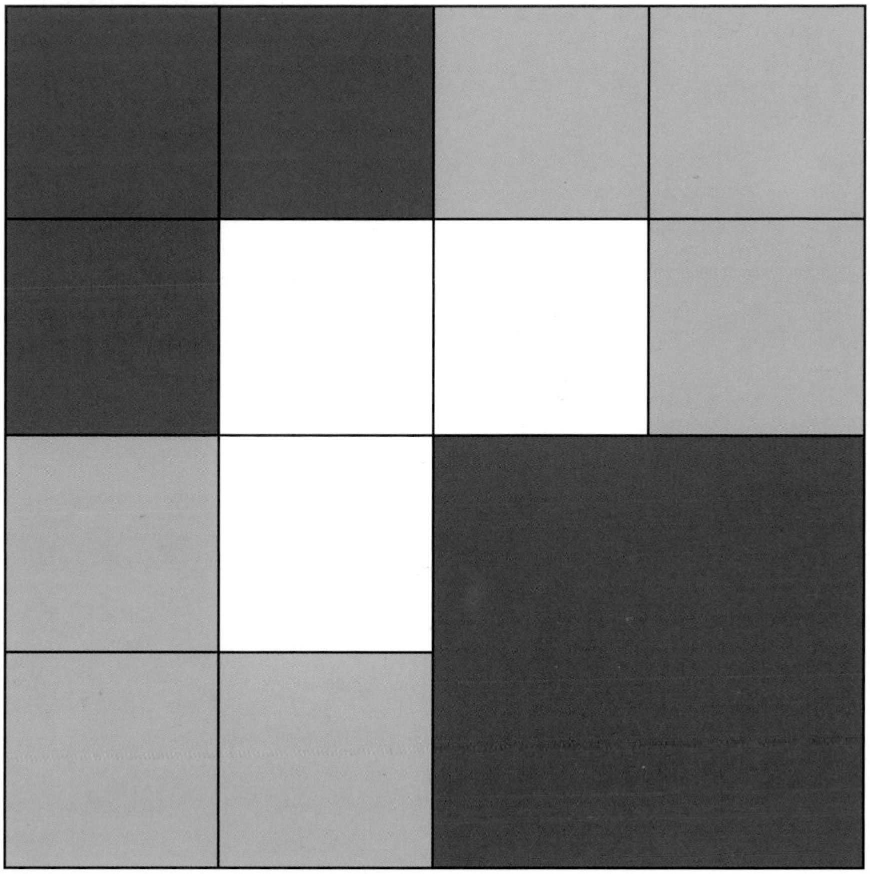

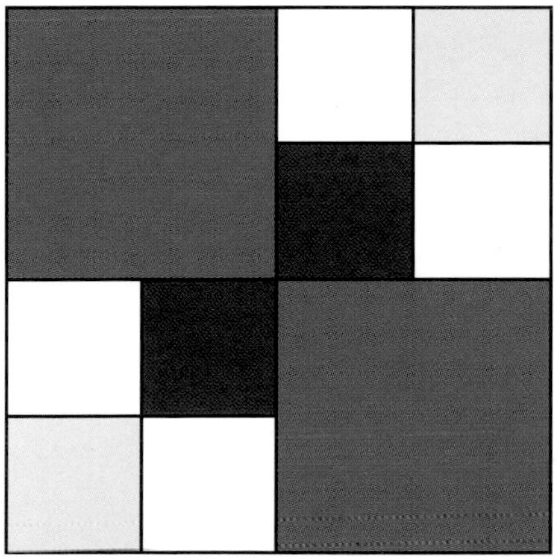

Ⓢ

Autumn Tint

block sizes 6", 8", 10"

2 – lg. squares, medium-dark
8 – sm. squares
　　4 light, 2 medium & 2 dark

Four-Patch

block sizes 6", 8", 10"

4 – lg. squares, light

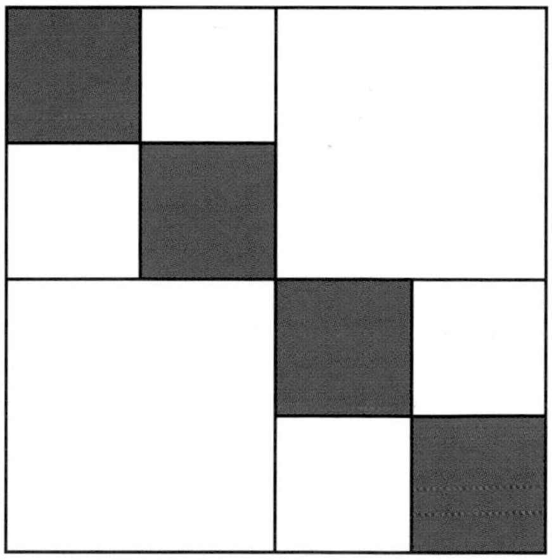

Ⓢ

Four-Patch

block sizes 6", 8", 10"

2 – lg. squares, light
8 – sm. squares
　　4 light & 4 dark

Ⓢ

easy

RAIL FENCE
Rosalba Kite
Kutztown, PA

Squares can appear as logs if the same fabric is used.

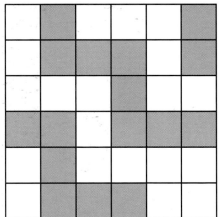

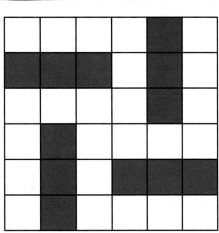

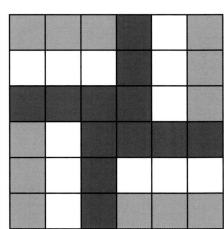

Fence Posts
two rail version
block size 12"

36 – sm. squares
   20 light & 16 medium

Fence Posts
three rail version
block size 12"

36 – sm. squares
   24 light & 12 dark

Rail Fence
three rail version
block size 12"

36 – sm. squares
   12 light, 12 medium &
   12 dark

BRIGHT HOPES

Debbie Welch
Bayville, NJ

Use old eye glass cases for storing your rotary cutters, always placing the blade end in first.

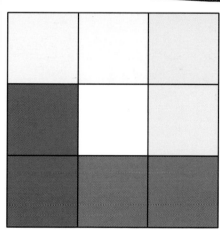

Bright Hopes
3 squares per rail
block sizes 6", 8", 10"

1 – lg. square, light
12 – sm. squares
    3 med-light, 3 medium,
    3 dark & 3 darker

Bright Hopes
2 squares per rail
block sizes 6", 9", 12"

9 – sm. squares
    1 light, 2 med-light,
    2 medium, 2 dark & 2 darker

Patience Corners
block sizes 6", 9", 12"

4 – lg. squares, light
20 – sm. squares, dark

SIMPLE NINE-PATCH

Pat Yamin
Brooklyn, NY

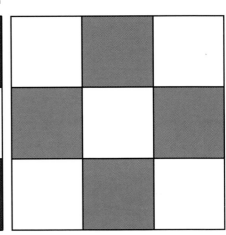

Album Quilt

block sizes 6", 9", 12"

9 – lg. squares
   1 light, 4 medium & 4 dark

Nine-Patch

block sizes 6", 9", 12"

9 – lg. squares
   4 light & 5 dark or
or
5 light & 4 dark

Simple Nine-Patch

block sizes 6", 9", 12"

9 – lg. squares
   5 light & 4 dark

Single Irish Chain

block sizes 6", 9", 12"

4 – lg. squares, light

45 – sm. squares
   20 light, 20 medium & 5 dark

Thrifty

block sizes 9", 12"

5 – lg. squares
   1 medium & 4 dark

16 – sm. squares
   8 light & 8 medium

Double Nine-Patch

block sizes 6", 9", 12"

8 – lg. squares
   4 light & 4 medium

9 – sm. squares
   4 light & 5 dark

Puss in the Corner

block sizes 9", 12"

4 – lg. squares, light

20 – sm. squares
   15 medium & 5 dark

West Wind Sail Boat

block sizes 6", 12"

2 – lg. half-sq. triangles
  1 light & 1 dark

10 – sm. half-sq. triangles
  5 light & 5 dark

how the blocks are placed together is called "setting." Try them stacked, or rotated to face inward or outward, to create the quilt you like the best. Notice the different placement positions below using four of the same block.

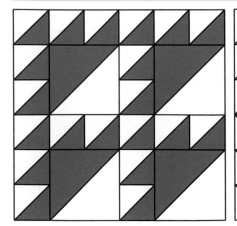

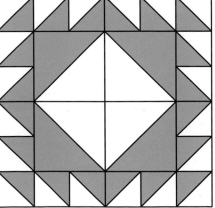

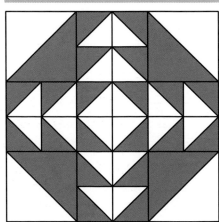

Pat Yamin ◆ **back** *to* BASICS

Indian Hatchet
block size 6", 8"

1 – lg. square, light
4 – sm. squares
   2 light & 2 dark
16 – sm. half-sq. triangles
   8 light & 8 dark

U se plastic sandwich bags that close to store the block pieces you are working on. Include the cut pieces of fabric, a sketch of the pattern, thread, needles, a couple of straight pins, a thimble, and a small pair of scissors.

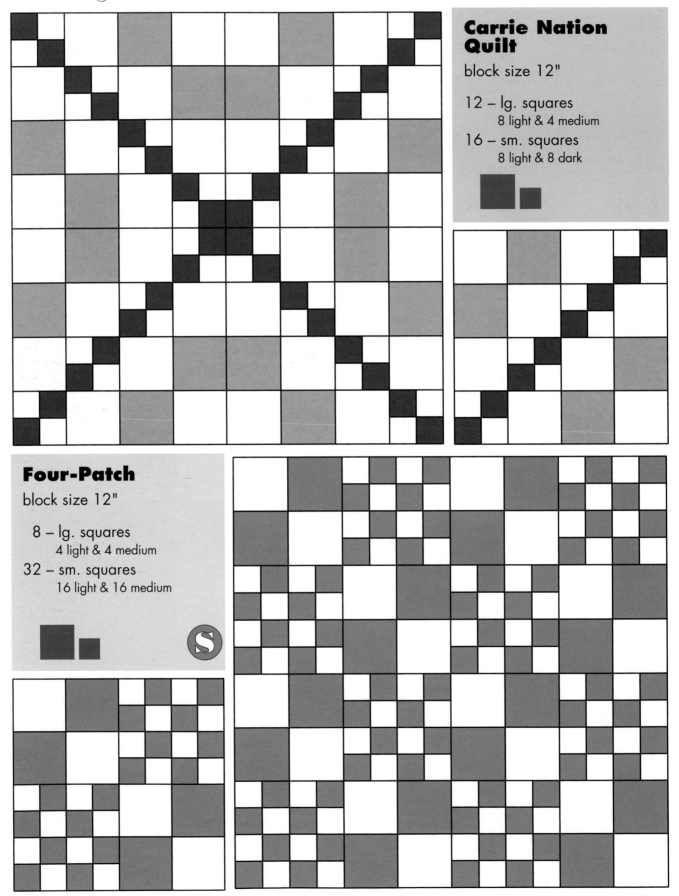

Carrie Nation Quilt

block size 12"

12 – lg. squares
  8 light & 4 medium

16 – sm. squares
  8 light & 8 dark

Four-Patch

block size 12"

8 – lg. squares
  4 light & 4 medium

32 – sm. squares
  16 light & 16 medium

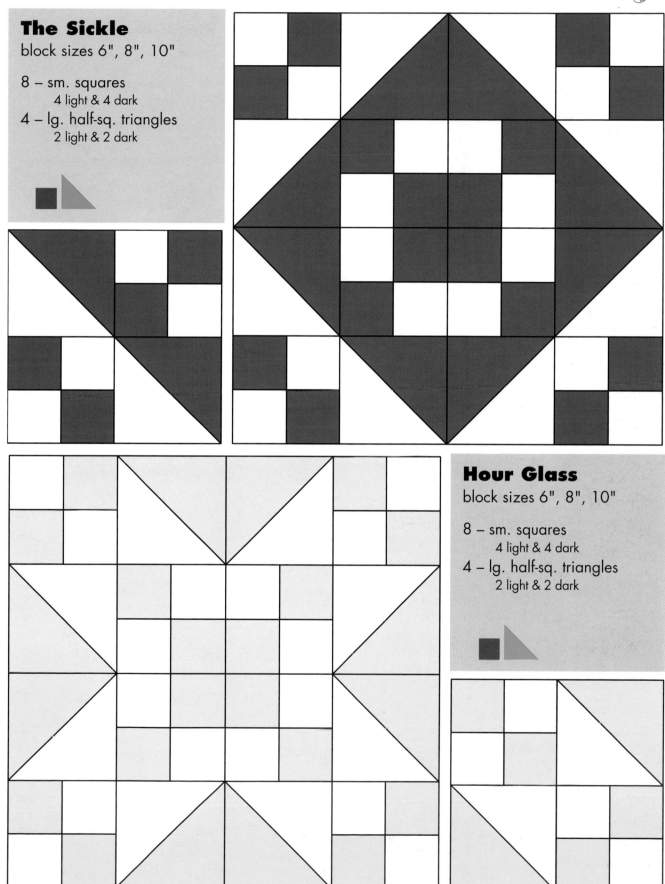

The Sickle
block sizes 6", 8", 10"

8 – sm. squares
    4 light & 4 dark
4 – lg. half-sq. triangles
    2 light & 2 dark

Hour Glass
block sizes 6", 8", 10"

8 – sm. squares
    4 light & 4 dark
4 – lg. half-sq. triangles
    2 light & 2 dark

easy

Road to Heaven
block sizes 6", 8", 10"

4 – sm. squares, dark
2 – lg. half-sq. triangles
   medium
16 – sm. half-sq. triangles
   10 light & 6 medium

always buy more fabric than you think you will use. Sometimes there are manufacturing flaws or you cut the wrong patch. If you are using black, navy, or dark green, you can never have enough yardage.

take a small portable light to class. If it is battery-charged, that is even better! You can never be sure that there will be enough good lighting in the classroom.

SQUARE IN A SQUARE

Rita Rehm
Hebron, CT

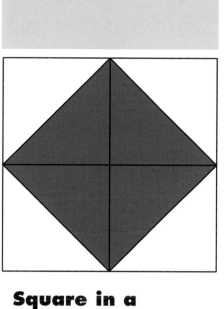

Square in a Square
Small Triangle Quilt

block sizes 6", 8", 10"

8 – lg. half-sq. triangles
4 light & 4 medium

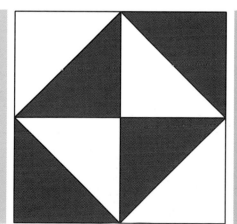

Broken Dishes
The Double Square

block sizes 6", 8", 10"

8 – lg. half-sq. triangles
4 light & 4 dark

Envelope
16-patch
block sizes 6", 8", 10", 12"

64 – quarter-sq. triangles
32 light & 32 dark

Use your address labels on your templates. When you take them to class, you will always get your templates back.

Big Dipper
Hour Glass
Bow Ties
2 colors
block sizes 6", 8", 10"

16 – quarter-sq. triangles
8 light & 8 dark

Envelope
Spinning Wheel
3 colors
block sizes 6", 8", 10"

16 – quarter-sq. triangles
8 light, 4 medium & 4 dark

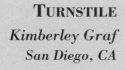

TURNSTILE
Kimberley Graf
San Diego, CA

Turnstile
block sizes 6", 8", 10"

4 – lg. half-sq. triangles
   light

8 – sm. quarter-sq. triangles
   4 medium & 4 dark

Turnstile on Pinwheels

Diane Hedrick
Perris, CA

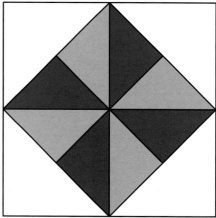

Pinwheel

2 colors

block sizes 6", 8", 10"

4 – lg. half-sq. triangles
   light

8 – med. half-sq. triangles
   4 medium & 4 dark

If someone has given you a bag of scraps that are musty or smell of smoke, place them in a pillow-case with a couple of bars of your favorite soap and tie it closed with a ribbon. In a week they will smell lovely.

Pinwheels

block sizes 6", 8", 10", 12"

4 – quarter-sq. triangles
  dark

8 – sm. half-sq. triangles
  medium

8 – sm. squares, light

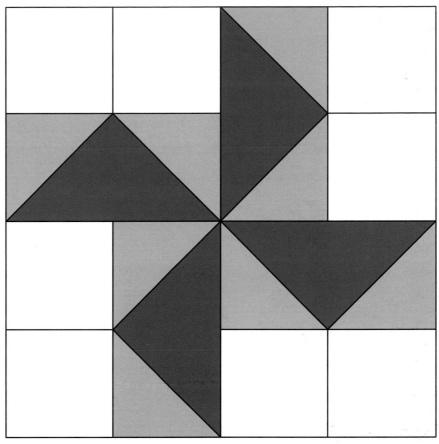

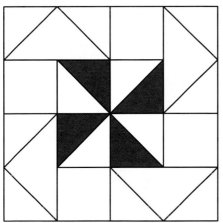

See Saw

block sizes 6", 8", 10", 12"

4 – quarter-sq. triangles
  medium

16 – sm. half-sq. triangles
  12 light & 4 dark

4 – sm. squares, light

make a test block of the block you want for your quilt. This will help you to understand the color arrangements, check your patterns, and help you to decide if you really like this block enough to sew fifty more!

extension cords always come in handy if you are at a friend's house sharing the electricity while working on a project. A power strip is even better.

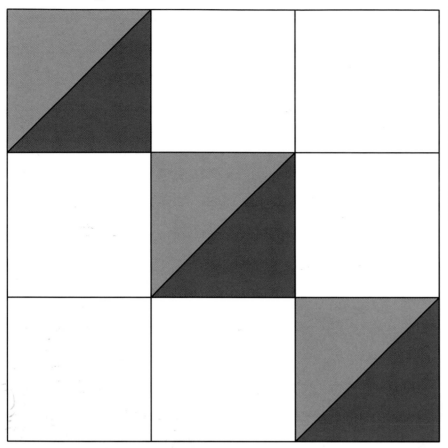

Trio

block sizes 6", 9", 12"

6 – lg. squares, light
6 – lg. half-sq. triangles
   3 medium & 3 dark

a great way to test your block is to make a full size drawing of it. Take it to the local print shop and make extra copies. Then you can use colored pencils or actually cut out fabric pieces and glue stick them in place to "audition" your color choices.

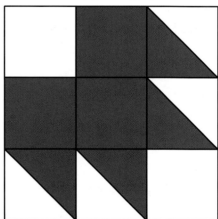

Tea Leaves

block sizes 6", 9", 12"

5 – lg. squares
   2 light & 3 medium
8 – lg. half-sq. triangles
   4 light & 4 medium

h ave an idea file of your next projects…these can come from any magazine. Sometimes even gardening magazines have great color combinations you can use for fabric ideas.

FRIENDSHIP STAR

Janet Graf
San Diego, CA

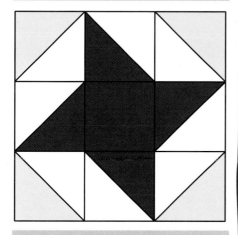

Indiana Puzzle
Friendship Star
Milky Way
Pinwheels

block sizes 6", 9", 12"

1 – lg. square, dark
16 – lg. half-sq. triangles
    8 light, 4 medium & 4 dark

if you are cutting fabric using a pair of scissors, make sure they are sharp and that you can evenly cut without getting choppy cut marks along the fabric edge.

easy

FRIENDSHIP STAR
Margrette Carr
San Diego, CA

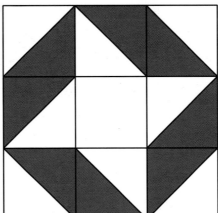

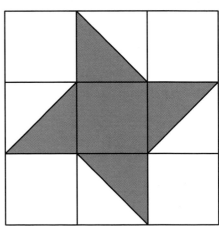

Quartered Star
3 colors

block sizes 6", 9", 12"

1 – lg. square, light
16 – lg. half-sq. triangles
8 light, 4 medium & 4 dark

Zig Zag Path
2 colors

block sizes 6", 9", 12"

1 – lg. square, light
16 – lg. half-sq. triangles
8 light & 8 dark

Friendship Star
2 colors

block sizes 6", 9", 12"

5 – lg. squares
4 light & 1 dark
8 – lg. half-sq. triangles
4 light & 4 dark

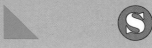

Friendly Hand
Indiana Puzzle
2 colors

block size 12"

  1 – lg. square, light

16 – sm. squares
     8 light & 8 dark

  8 – lg. half-sq. triangles
     4 light & 4 dark

Milky Way
3 colors

block size 12"

  4 – lg. squares
     2 light & 2 medium

16 – sm. squares
     8 light & 8 dark

16 – lg. half-sq. triangles
     8 light & 8 medium

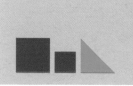

easy

PHILADELPHIA

Diane Weber
Cupertino, CA

be sure to pay attention to matching the seams. Finger pressing while you sew is usually the best way to achieve accuracy.

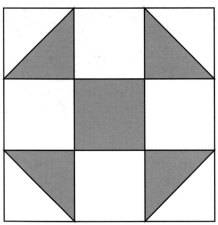

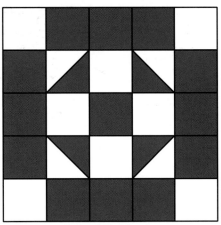

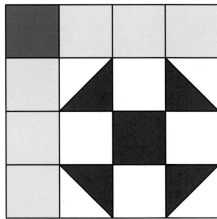

Shoo-fly

block sizes 6", 9", 12"

5 – lg. squares
    4 light & 1 dark
8 – lg. half-sq. triangles
    4 light & 4 dark

Philadelphia Pavement

block size 10"

21 – lg. squares
    8 light & 13 dark
8 – lg. half-sq. triangles
    4 light, 4 dark

Philadelphia

block sizes 6", 8", 10", 12"

12 – lg. squares
    4 light, 6 medium-light,
    1 medium & 1 dark
8 – lg. half-sq. triangles
    4 light & 4 dark

CARD TRICK
Marge Geary
Williston Park, NY

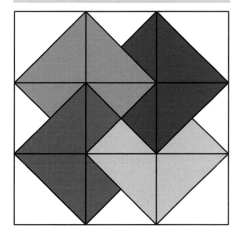

Card Trick
Crow's Nest
block sizes 9", 12"

12 – half-sq. triangles
   4 light, 2 medium-light
   2 medium, 2 medium-dark
   & 2 dark

12 – quarter-sq. triangles
   4 light, 2 medium-light
   2 medium, 2 medium-dark
   & 2 dark

Wrapped Packages
block sizes 9", 12"

12 – half-sq. triangles
   4 light, 4 medium & 4 dark
12 – quarter-sq. triangles
   4 light, 2 medium & 6 dark

RAINBOW
Linda Denner
Warrensburg, NY

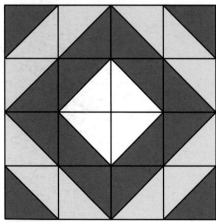

When using rotary cutters, save the old blades carefully in a container marked "used." These are great to use when cutting wallpaper, coupons, or for paper craft projects.

Depression
block sizes 6", 8", 12"

32 – lg. half-sq. triangles
    4 light, 12 medium, &
    16 dark

remember: There is only one blade used in your rotary cutter. Yes, the 28mm is packaged two blades in a package, but they are meant to be used one at a time!

Flying Goose

block sizes 8", 10"

1 – lg. half-sq., light
4 – sm. half-sq.
    1 light & 3 medium

Flying Geese

block sizes 8", 10"

  4 – lg. half-sq. triangles
    light
16 – sm. half-sq. triangles
    4 light & 12 medium

Trade Off

block sizes 8", 10"

  4 – lg. half-sq. triangles
    2 light & 2 dark
16 – sm. half-sq. triangles
    8 light, 6 medium & 2 dark

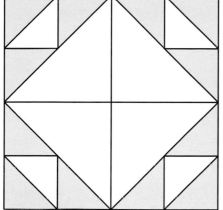

early in the morning thread at least twenty needles on a spool of thread. The light is better and you won't have to wait for the kids to come home to help.

WAMPUM BLOCK

Diane Weber
Cupertino, CA

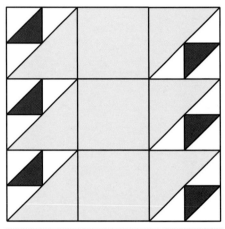

WAMPUM BLOCK

Margrette Carr
San Diego, CA

Wampum Block

block sizes 9", 12"

- 3 – lg. squares, medium
- 6 – lg. half- sq. triangles
  medium
- 24 – sm. half- sq. triangles
  18 light & 6 dark

Wampum Block

block sizes 9", 12"

- 3 – lg. squares, 1 light & 2 dark
- 6 – lg. half- sq. triangles
  medium
- 24 – sm. half- sq. triangles
  18 light & 6 dark

The Arkansas Crossroads

block sizes 6", 8", 12"

12 – lg. squares
    4 light, 4 medium-light
    & 4 dark
8 – lg. half-sq. triangles
    4 light & 4 medium

Pinwheel
Paper Pinwheels

block sizes 6", 8", 12"

12 – lg. squares
    4 light, 4 medium & 4 dark
8 – lg. half-sq. triangles
    4 light & 4 medium

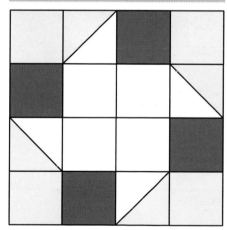

Road to Oklahoma

block sizes 6", 8", 12"

12 – lg. squares
    6 light & 6 dark
8 – lg. half-sq. triangles
    4 light & 4 dark

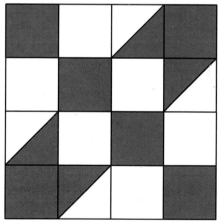

The Anvil

block sizes 6", 8", 12"

8 – lg. squares
    4 light & 4 dark
16 – lg. half-sq. triangles
    8 light & 8 dark

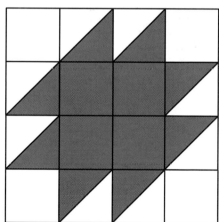

Crow's Feet
block sizes 6", 9", 12"

4 – lg. squares, 2 light & 2 dark

4 – sm. squares
2 light & 2 dark

32 – sm. half-sq. triangles
16 light & 16 dark

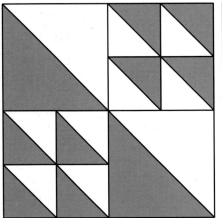

Flock of Geese
block sizes 6", 8", 10"

4 – lg. half-sq. triangles
2 light & 2 dark

16 – sm. half-sq. triangles
8 light & 8 dark

Flock of Geese
block sizes 6", 8", 10"

32 – sm. squares
16 light & 16 medium

16 – lg. half-sq. triangles
8 light & 8 dark

Wagon Tracks
Pacific Railroad
block sizes 9", 12"

20 – sm. squares
10 light & 10 medium

8 – lg. half-sq. triangles
4 light & 4 dark

back *to* BASICS ◆ Pat Yamin

Jacob's Ladder
2 colors

block sizes 9", 12"

20 – sm. squares
   10 light & 10 medium
8 – lg. half-sq. triangles
   4 light & 4 medium

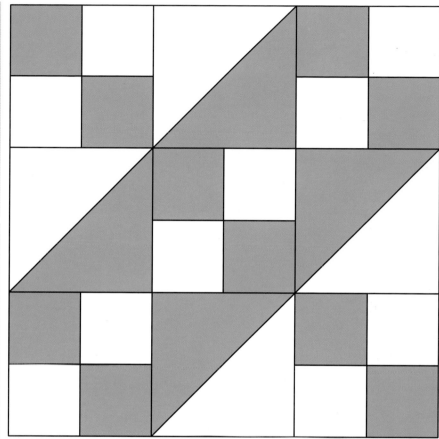

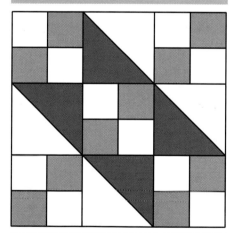

Jacob's Ladder
3 colors

block sizes 9", 12"

20 – sm. squares
   10 light & 10 medium
8 – lg. half-sq. triangles
   4 light & 4 dark

Jacob's Ladder
star

block sizes 9", 12"

20 – sm. squares
   8 light, 6 medium & 6 dark
8 – lg. half-sq. triangles
   4 light & 4 medium

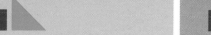

Jacob's Ladder
variation

block sizes 9", 12"

12 – sm. squares
   6 light & 6 medium
12 – lg. half-sq. triangles
   6 light & 6 medium

Old Maid's Puzzle
2 colors

block sizes 6", 8", 10"

4 – sm. squares, light
2 – lg. half-sq. triangles, dark
16 – sm. half-sq. triangles
   10 light & 6 dark

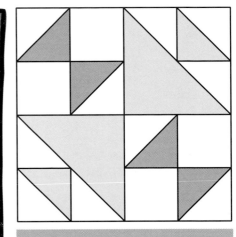

Old Maid's Puzzle
3 colors

block sizes 6", 8", 10"

4 – sm. squares, light
2 – lg. half-sq. triangles, med.
16 – sm. half-sq. triangles
   10 light, 2 medium & 4 dark

OLD MAID'S PUZZLE

Judith Klein
Flushing, NY

Whirligig

block sizes 6", 8", 10"

24 – lg. half-sq. triangle
    8 light & 16 dark
 4 – lg. quarter-sq. triangles
    light

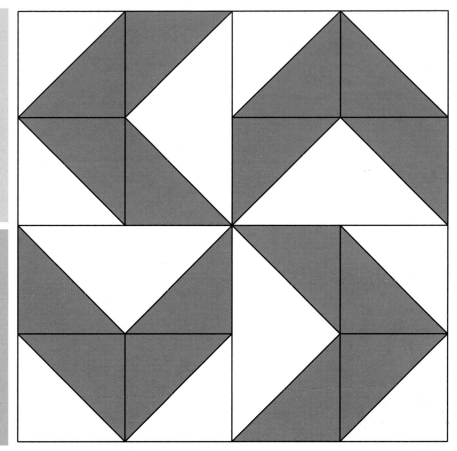

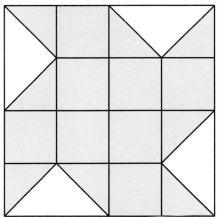

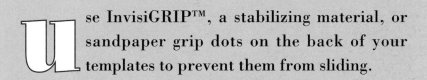

Use InvisiGRIP™, a stabilizing material, or sandpaper grip dots on the back of your templates to prevent them from sliding.

Churn Dash

block sizes 6", 8"

8 – sm. squares, dark
8 – sm. half-sq. triangles
    dark
4 – sm. quarter-sq. triangles
    light

With all of the scraps you have at the end of the day, take five more minutes and cut them into 2" or 3" squares.

Caged Pinwheel

block sizes 6", 8", 10"

4 – sm. squares, medium
4 – lg. half-sq. triangles
medium
8 – sm. half-sq. triangles
4 light & 4 dark

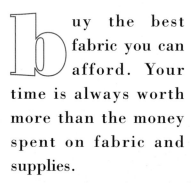

buy the best fabric you can afford. Your time is always worth more than the money spent on fabric and supplies.

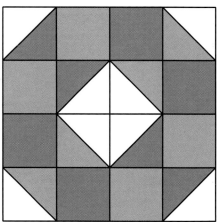

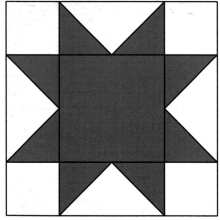

Sawtooth Star
Square and Point

block sizes 6", 8", 10"

1 – lg. square, dark
4 – sm. squares, light
8 – sm. half-sq. triangles, dark
4 – lg. quarter-sq.triangles, light

Indian Star

block sizes 6", 8", 10"

8 – small squares
2 light & 6 medium
8 – sm. half-sq. triangles, dark
4 – lg. quarter-sq. triangles
light

Cheyenne

block sizes 6", 8", 10", 12"

8 – sm. squares
4 medium & 4 dark
16 – sm. half-sq. triangles
8 light, 4 medium & 4 dark

KING'S CROWN
Madalene Becker
Edgewater, CO

Save time by stacking at least four strips of fabric to cut together.

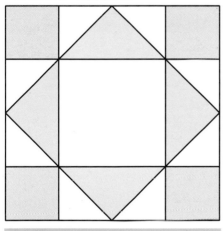

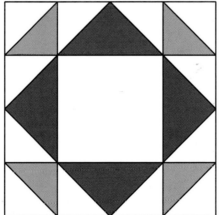

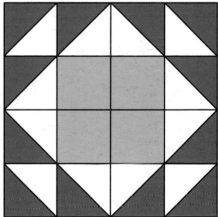

King's Crown
block sizes 6", 8", 10"

1 – lg. square, light
4 – sm. squares, medium
8 – sm. half-sq. triangles, light
4 – lg. quarter-sq. triangles dark

The Cypress
block sizes 8", 10"

1 – lg. square, light
16 – sm. half-sq. triangle
    12 light & 4 medium
4 – lg. quarter-sq. triangles dark

Sweet Promises
block sizes 6", 8", 10", 12"

4 – sm. squares, medium
24 – sm. half-sq. triangle
    12 light & 12 dark

MISSOURI STAR

Diane Weber
Cupertino, CA

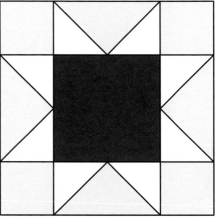

Missouri Star

block sizes 6", 8", 10"

1 – lg. square, dark
4 – sm. squares, medium
8 – sm. half-sq. triangles, light
4 – lg. quarter-sq. triangles
    medium

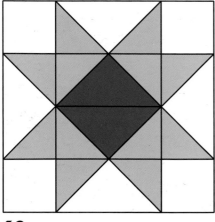

Missouri Star

block sizes 6", 8", 10"

4 – sm. squares, light
12 – sm. half-sq. triangles
    medium
6 – lg. quarter-sq. triangles
    4 light & 2 dark

an oilcloth table cover with a flannel backing works well for laying out your quilting project. Use the flannel side face up to audition your quilt blocks.

back *to* BASICS ◆ Pat Yamin

Queen's Crown
2 colors

block size 10"

7 – sm. squares, 6 light & 1 dark
2 – lg. half-sq. triangles, dark
28 – sm. half-sq. triangles
16 light & 12 dark

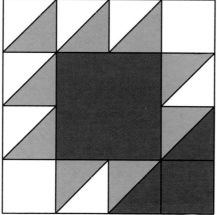

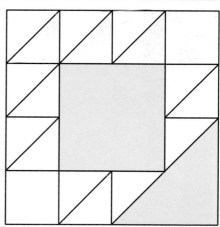

Queen's Crown
3 colors
block size 10"

7 – sm. squares
2 light, 4 medium & 1 dark
2 – lg. half-sq. triangles
28 – sm. half-sq. triangles
8 light, 8 medium & 12 dark

The Swallow
variation

block sizes 6", 8", 10"

1 – lg. square, dark
3 – sm. squares, 2 light &1 dark
18 – sm. half-sq. triangles
7 light, 9 medium & 2 dark

The Swallow

block sizes 6", 8", 10"

1 – lg. square, dark
2 – sm. squares, light
1 – lg. half-sq. triangle, dark
16 – sm. half-sq. triangles
7 light & 9 medium

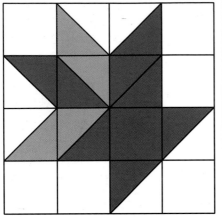

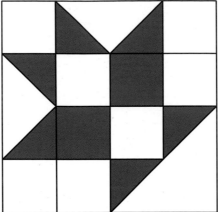

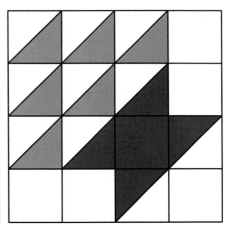

Flower Basket

block sizes 6", 8", 10", 12"

7 – sm. squares
6 light & 1 dark
18 – sm. half-sq. triangles
6 light, 4 medium-light
4 medium & 4 dark

Baby Bunting

block sizes 6", 8", 10"

1 – lg. half-sq. triangle, light
2 – lg. quarter-sq. triangles, light
9 – sm. squares
7 light & 2 dark
6 – sm. half-sq. triangles, dark

Simple Flower Basket

block sizes 6", 8", 10", 12"

6 – sm. squares
5 light & 1 dark
20 – sm. half-sq. triangles
10 light, 6 medium & 4 dark

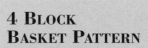

4 BLOCK BASKET PATTERN

Sandy Brown
Spokane, WA

FRUIT BASKET

Marge Geary
Williston Park, NY

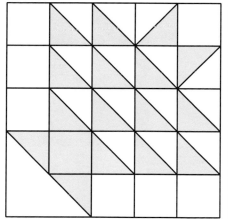

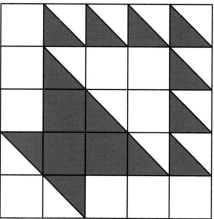

Fruit Basket

block size 10"

1 – lg. half-sq. triangle, light

8 – sm. squares
  7 light & 1 dark

30 – sm. half-sq. triangles
  14 light & 16 dark

Fruit Basket

block size 10"

13 – sm. squares
  10 light & 3 dark

24 – sm. half-sq. triangles
  12 light & 12 dark

Bea's Basket

block size 10"

3 – lg. half-sq. triangles, light

6 – sm. squares, light

18 – sm. half-sq. triangles
  10 light & 8 dark

16 – sm. quarter-sq. triangles
  12 light & 4 dark

Hour Glass

block size 6"

1 – sm. square, dark
2 – lg. half-sq. triangles, medium
8 – sm. half-sq. triangles
   6 light & 2 dark

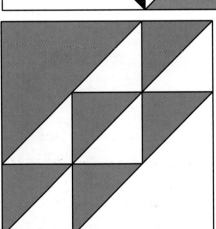

Corn & Beans Simple Design

block size 6"

2 – lg. half-sq. triangles
   1 light & 1 dark
10 – sm. half-sq. triangles
   5 light & 5 dark

Double X

block sizes 6", 9", 12"

18 – sm. half-sq. triangles
   12 light & 6 dark

Split Nine-Patch

block sizes 6", 9", 12"

18 – sm. half-sq. triangles
   10 light & 8 dark

Boy's Nonsense

block sizes 6", 9", 12"

1 – large square, medium
8 – lg. half-square triangles
   4 light & 4 medium
16 – sm. quarter-sq. triangles
   8 light & 8 medium

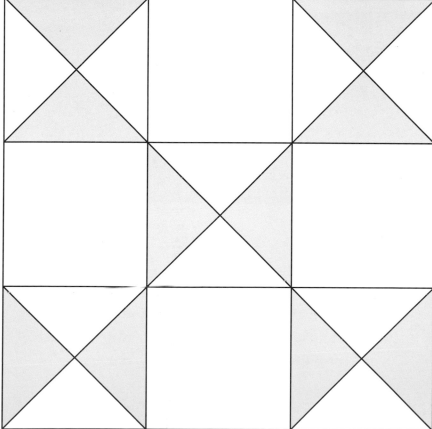

se suction cups on a ruler longer than 12". Then walk your fingers up the ruler to keep control so it doesn't wobble and shift as you cut.

Flying X

block sizes 6", 9", 12"

4 – lg. squares, light
20 – sm. quarter-sq. triangles
   10 light & 10 dark

MONKEY WRENCH

Kimberley Graf
San Diego, CA

If your presser foot moves or has a mind of its own, buy a roll of the sponge shelving material used to line kitchen cupboards. Simply measure the size of your presser foot and cut a piece to slip underneath.

HOLE IN THE BARN DOOR

Judith Klein
Flushing, NY

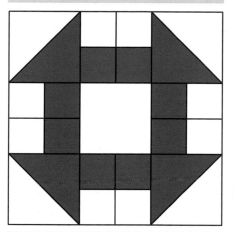

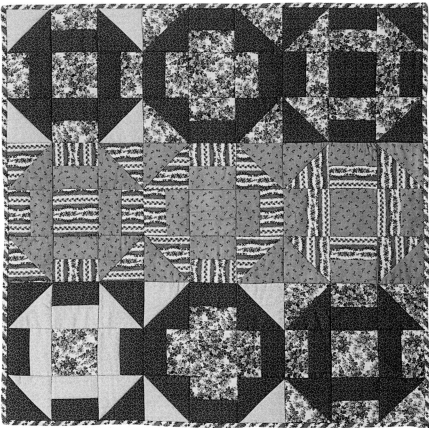

Churn Dash
Shoo-Fly
Monkey Wrench
Hole in the Barn Door

block sizes 9", 12"

  1 – lg. square, light
16 – sm. squares
        8 light & 8 dark
  8 – lg. half-sq. triangles
        4 light & 4 dark

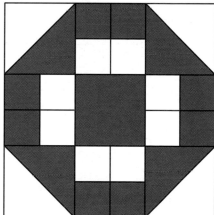

Grecian Design

block sizes 9", 12"

  1 – lg. square, dark
16 – sm. squares
        8 light & 8 dark
  8 – lg. half-sq. triangles
        4 light & 4 dark

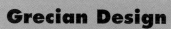

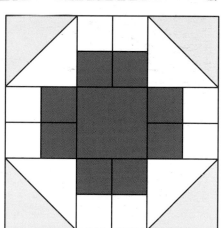

Greek Cross

block sizes 9", 12"

  1 – lg. square, dark
16 – sm. squares
        8 light & 8 dark
  8 – lg. half-sq. triangles
        4 light & 4 medium

Lone Star
Ohio Star
Eight Point Design
Star Design
Texas Star
Tippecanoe and Tyler Too
Texas
Eastern Star

2 colors

block sizes 6", 9", 12"

5 – lg. squares
   4 light & 1 dark
16 – lg. quarter-sq. triangles
   8 light & 8 dark

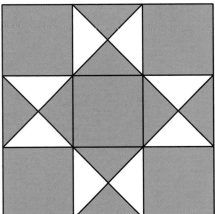

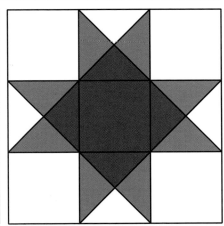

Aunt Eliza's Star
Aunt Lottie's Star
Texas Star

2 colors

block sizes 6", 9", 12"

5 – lg. squares, medium
16 – lg. quarter-sq. triangles
   8 light & 8 medium

Ohio Star

3 colors

block sizes 6", 9", 12"

5 – lg. squares
   4 light & 1 dark
16 – lg. quarter-sq. triangles
   4 light, 8 medium & 4 dark

Variable Star

4 colors

block sizes 6", 9", 12"

5 – lg. squares
   4 medium & 1 dark
16 – lg. quarter-sq. triangles
   4 light, 4 medium-light
   & 8 medium

OHIO STAR
Margrette Carr
San Diego, CA

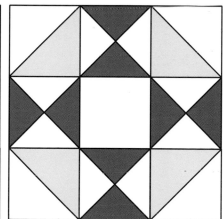

Mosaic Flying Crow
3 colors

block sizes 6", 9", 12"

5 – lg. squares, medium
16 – lg. quarter-sq. triangles
8 light & 8 dark

The Four-X Quilt
2 colors

block sizes 6", 9", 12"

1 – lg. square, medium
8 – lg. half-sq. triangles
4 light & 4 medium
16 – lg. quarter-sq. triangles
8 light & 8 medium

Swamp Angel
3 colors

block sizes 6", 9", 12"

1 – lg. square, light
8 – lg. half-sq. triangles
4 light & 4 medium
16 – lg. quarter-sq. triangles
8 light & 8 dark

Star X
The Silent Star
2 colors
block sizes 6", 9", 12"

8 – lg. half-sq. triangles
   4 light & 4 medium
20 – lg. quarter-sq. triangles
   10 light & 10 medium

after completing each seam, trim the threads close to the patchwork. Then they will not be in your way as you progress to blocks with a lot of pieces.

Four Corners
2 colors
block sizes 9", 12"

16 – sm. squares
   12 light & 4 medium
20 – lg. quarter-sq. triangles
   10 light & 10 medium

Rolling Square

block size 10"

9 – sm. squares, dark
32 – sm. half-sq. triangles
    16 light & 16 dark

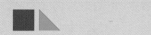

Lint brushes help to get all of those loose threads off you before company comes. You can also attach a lint roller to the end of a long pole to pick up loose threads from the floor.

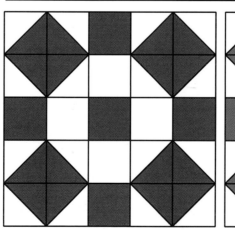

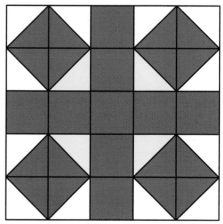

Rolling Square variation

block size 10"

9 – sm. squares
    4 light & 5 dark
32 – sm. half-sq. triangles
    16 light & 16 dark

Rolling Square variation

block size 10"

9 – sm. squares, dark
32 – sm. half-sq. triangles
    12 light, 4 medium & 16 dark

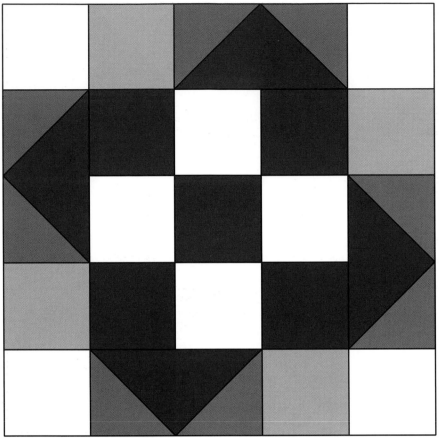

Rolling Nine-Patch
4 colors
block size 10"

17 – sm. squares
   8 light, 4 medium & 5 dark
8 – sm. half-sq. triangles
   medium-dark
4 – med. quarter-sq. triangles
   dark

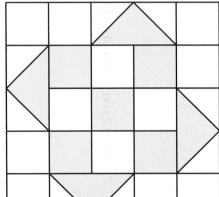

Rolling Nine-Patch
2 colors
block size 10"

17 – sm. squares
   12 light & 5 dark
8 – sm. half-sq. triangles
   light
4 – med. quarter-sq. triangles
   dark

Cups and Saucers
block sizes 9", 12"

1 – lg. square, medium
8 – lg. half-sq. triangles
   4 light & 4 medium
8 – lg. quarter-sq. triangles
   light
16 – sm. half-sq. triangles
   medium

Capital T
Double T
Cut the Corners
block sizes 9", 12"

1 – lg. square, light
8 – lg. half-sq. triangles, light
8 – lg. quarter-sq. triangles light
16 – sm. half-sq. triangles dark

Eight Point Star
block sizes 9", 12"

5 – lg. squares
4 light & 1 dark
8 – lg. quarter-sq. triangles
4 light & 4 dark
16 – sm. half-sq. triangles
8 light & 8 dark

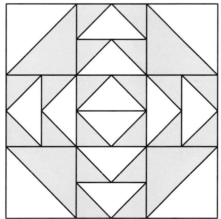

Illinois
block sizes 9", 12"

8 – lg. half-sq. triangles,
4 light & 4 dark
10 – lg. quarter-sq. triangles
light
20 – sm. half-sq. triangles
dark

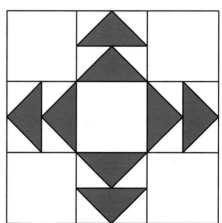

North, South, East, West
block sizes 9", 12"

5 – lg. squares, light
8 – lg. quarter-sq. triangles medium
16 – sm. half-sq. triangles light

T Quilt

Margrette Carr
San Diego, CA

I have always liked this pattern for its simple yet interesting arrangements of blocks. I also have a strong tie to this popular pattern, as my maiden name was Tidmore.

The T Quilt

block sizes 6", 12"

4 – lg. half-sq. triangles, light
4 – sm. squares, dark
48 – sm. half-sq. triangles
  20 light & 28 dark

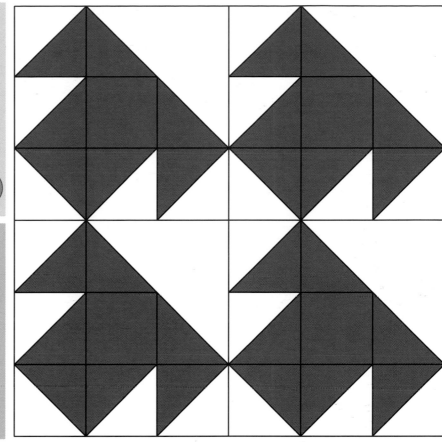

T Blocks

block sizes 6", 9", 12"

4 – lg. half-sq. triangles, light
4 – sm. squares, dark
48 – sm. half-sq. triangles
  20 light & 28 dark

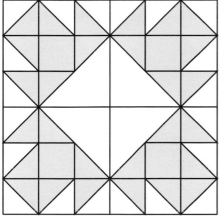

Four T's

block sizes 9", 12"

4 – lg. half-sq. triangles, light
10 – lg. quarter-sq. triangles
  light
4 – sm. squares, dark
28 – sm. half-sq. triangles, dark

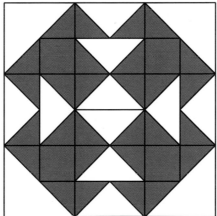

Imperial T

block sizes 9", 12"

8 – lg. half-sq. triangles
  4 light & 4 dark
10 – lg. quarter-sq. triangles
  light
20 – sm. half-sq. triangles, dark

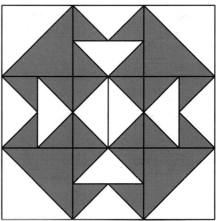

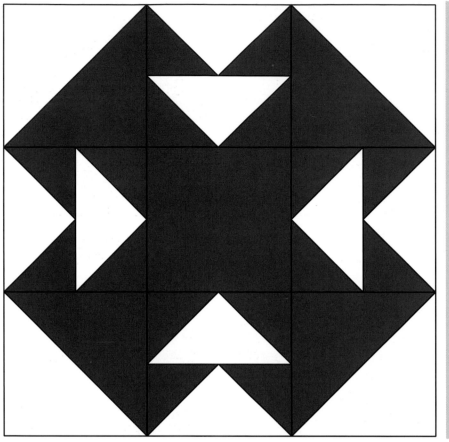

Double T
Four T Square
Capital T
Friendship Quilt

block sizes 9", 12"

1 – lg. square, dark

8 – lg. half-sq. triangles
4 light & 4 dark

8 – lg. quarter-sq. triangles
light

16 – sm. half-sq. triangles
dark

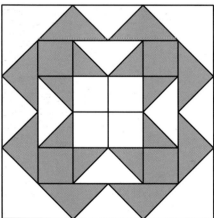

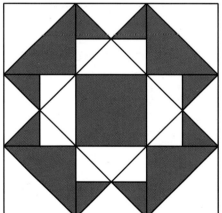

The T Quilt Pattern
block sizes 9", 12"

4 – lg. half-sq. triangles, light

16 – lg. quarter-sq. triangles
8 light & 8 dark

8 – sm. squares
4 light & 4 dark

8 – sm. half-sq. triangles, dark

Four T's
block sizes 9", 12"

1 – lg. square, dark

8 – lg. half-sq. triangles
4 light & 4 dark

8 – lg. quarter-sq. triangles
light

16 – sm. half-sq. triangles
8 light & 8 dark

Capital T
block sizes 9", 12"

1 – lg. square, light

8 – lg. half-sq. triangles
4 light & 4 dark

8 – lg. quarter-sq. triangles
light

16 – sm. half-sq. triangles, dark

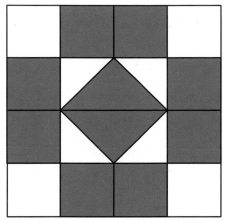

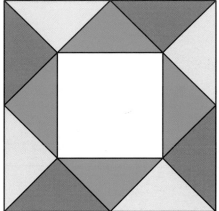

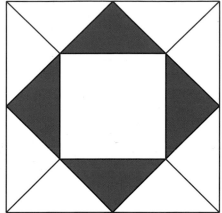

New Album

2 colors

block sizes 6", 8", 12"

12 – sm. squares
    4 light & 8 dark
4 – sm. half-sq. triangles, light
2 – lg. quarter-sq. triangles
    dark

Economy Patch
Hour Glass

4 colors

block sizes 6", 8", 10"

1 – lg. square, light
12 – lg. quarter-sq. triangles
    4 medium-light, 4 medium
    & 4 dark

Thrift Patch
This and That

2 colors

block sizes 6", 8", 10"

1 – lg. square, light
12 – lg. quarter-sq. triangles
    8 light & 4 dark

Square on Square
Scrap

block size 8"

4 – lg. half-sq. triangles, dark
4 – lg. quarter-sq. triangles
    light
4 – med. half-sq. triangles
    dark
4 – med. quarter-sq. triangles
    light
8 – sm. half-sq. triangles
    4 light & 4 dark

Next Door Neighbor
3 colors
block sizes 6", 8", 10"

12 – med. quarter-sq. triangles
    4 light, 4 medium & 4 dark
4 – sm. half-sq. triangles, light
4 – sm. quarter-sq. triangles
    2 medium & 2 dark

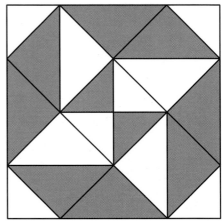

Next Door Neighbor Square Up
2 colors
block sizes 6", 8", 10"

12 – med. quarter-sq. triangles
    4 light & 8 dark
4 – sm. half-sq. triangles, light
4 – sm. quarter-sq. triangles
    2 light & 2 dark

did you buy too much of that lovely purple fabric? Cut it into fat quarters, wrap it with a pretty ribbon, and give it to the next new guild member you meet.

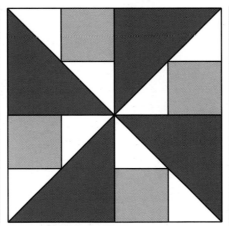

Brave World
block sizes 6", 8", 10"

4 – lg. half-sq. triangles
    dark
4 – sm. squares, medium
8 – sm. half-sq. triangles
    light

ACROBATS

Madalene Becker
Edgewater, CO

the templates in the book on pages 103–108 have double cut corners, so there will not be any "dog-ears" on any of your patches.

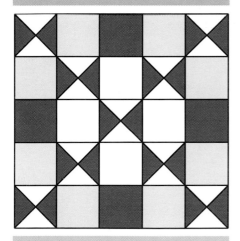

Acrobats

block size 10"

16 – sm. squares
    4 light, 8 medium & 4 dark
36 – sm. quarter-sq. triangles
    18 light & 18 dark

Handy Andy Foot Stool
2 colors

block size 10"

 9 – sm. squares, light

24 – sm. half-sq. triangles
   12 light & 12 dark

16 – sm. quarter-sq. triangles
   8 light & 8 dark

Clown
3 colors

block size 10"

14 – sm. squares, light

44 – sm. quarter-sq. triangles
   22 light, 11 medium & 11 dark

Caroline's Choice

block sizes 6", 8", 10"

8 – med quarter-sq. triangles
light

16 – sm. half-sq. triangles
8 light & 8 dark

Dutchman's Puzzle

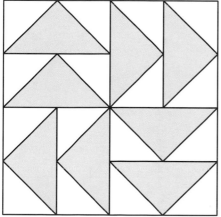

block sizes 6", 8", 10"

8 – lg. quarter-sq. triangle
dark

16 – sm. half-sq. triangles
light

Mosaic #12
Mosaic #9
Mosaic #5

block sizes 6", 8", 10"

8 – lg. quarter-sq. triangle
dark

16 – sm. half-sq. triangles
light

a s a teacher, I always pack band aids with my supplies. A new rotary blade can give a student a deep cut without even knowing it.

Old English
Wedding Ring
Wedding Ring

block size 10"

9 – sm. squares
   4 light & 5 dark
32 – sm. half-sq. triangles
   16 light & 16 dark

Design in
Geometrics

block sizes 6", 8", 10"

4 – lg. quarter-sq. triangle
   2 light & 2 dark
8 – sm. squares, medium
16 – sm. quarter-sq. triangles
   8 light & 8 dark

THE ANVIL
Laura Lipski
Lindenhurst, NY

Spinning Jenny

4 colors

block sizes 6", 8", 10"

16 – lg. quarter-sq. triangles
2 light, 2 medium-light,
8 medium & 4 dark

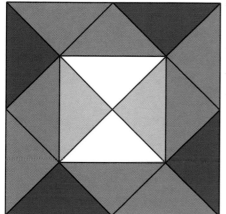

piecing diagram

The Anvil

block sizes 8", 10"

1 – lg. square, dark
2 – sm. squares, light
2 – lg. half-sq. triangles, light
12 – sm. half-sq. triangles
4 light & 8 dark

Boise

3 colors

block sizes 6", 8", 10"

10 – lg. quarter-sq. triangles
2 light, 4 medium & 4 dark
4 – sm. squares, medium
4 – sm. half-sq. triangles, light

advanced

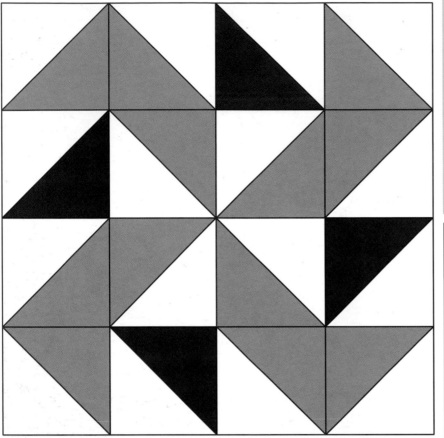

Ring Around the Rosy

3 colors

block sizes 6", 8", 10", 12"

32 – sm. half-sq. triangles
16 light, 12 medium & 4 dark

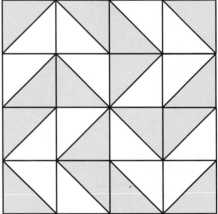

Fly Foot
Winding Blades
Devil's Puzzle
Indian Emblem
Catch Me If You
Can

2 colors

block sizes 6", 8", 10", 12"

32 – sm. half-sq. triangles
16 light & 16 dark

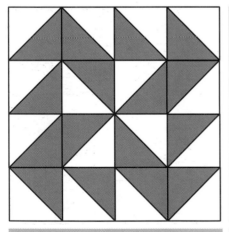

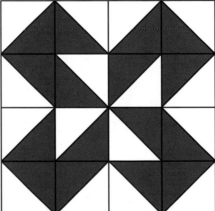

Yankee Puzzle

2 colors

block sizes 6", 8", 10", 12"

32 – sm. half-sq. triangles
16 light & 16 dark

Big Dipper

2 colors

block sizes 6", 8", 10", 12"

32 – sm. half-sq. triangles
16 light & 16 dark

4X STAR

Linda Denner
Warrensburg, NY

Four X Star

2 colors

block size 10"

17 – sm. squares
8 light & 9 medium
16 – sm. half-sq. triangles
8 light & 8 dark

Four X Star

3 colors

block size 10"

17 – sm. squares
8 light, 8 medium & 1 dark
16 – sm. half-sq. triangles
8 light & 8 dark

Father's Day

3 colors

block size 10"

17 – sm. squares
8 light, 4 medium & 5 dark
16 – sm. half-sq. triangles
8 light & 8 medium

WEDDING RING

Lucy McCandless
Spokane, WA

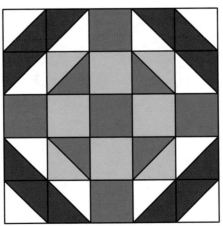

chain stitch when-ever possible. This not only saves thread, but it saves time.

Wedding Ring
4 colors
block size 10"

9 – sm. squares
   4 medium-light & 5 medium
32 – sm. half-sq. triangles
   12 light, 4 medium-light
   4 medium & 12 dark

Wedding Ring
block size 10"

9 – sm. squares
   5 light & 4 medium-light
32 – sm. half-sq. triangles
   16 light, 8 medium & 8 dark

back *to* **BASICS** ◆ Pat Yamin

Wedding Ring

3 colors

block size 10"

- 9 – sm. squares
  - 5 medium & 4 dark
- 16 – sm. half-sq. triangles
  - 12 light & 4 dark
- 8 – sm. quarter-sq. triangles
  - dark

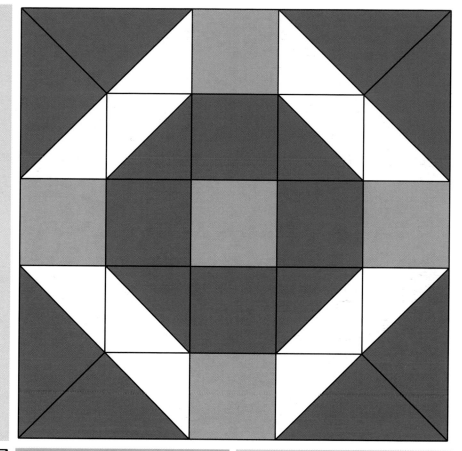

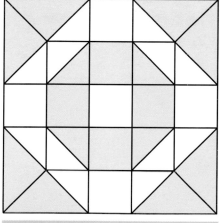

Wedding Ring

2 colors

block size 10"

- 9 – sm. squares
  - 5 light & 4 dark
- 16 – sm. half-sq. triangles
  - 12 light & 4 dark
- 8 – med. quarter-sq. triangles
  - dark

finger-press the pieces as you sew and then, when the block is finished, you can lightly iron it from the wrong side.

never keep your template plastic rolled up. As soon as possible, unroll it and lay it flat or stand it up next to your sewing table.

Wheel of Fortune
block size 10"

9 – sm. squares, dark
32 – sm. half-sq. triangles
16 light & 16 dark

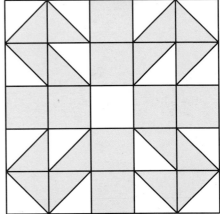

Use an opened coat hanger to store your leftover bias tape. I wrap the bias tape around cardboard from paper rolls and this cylinder fits the hanger perfectly.

Jack in the Box
Whirligig
Wheel of Chance
block size 10"

9 – sm. squares
    1 light & 8 dark
32 – sm. half-sq. triangles
    16 light & 16 dark

buy a roll of black and white film, (12–24 shots) to take pictures of your project. You will be able to see the color contrast quickly in the developed photographs.

Castles in Spain

block sizes 6", 8", 10"

10 – lg. quarter-sq. triangles
   6 light & 4 dark
12 – sm. half-sq. triangles
   4 light & 8 dark

Double Cross

block sizes 6", 8", 10"

14 – lg. quarter-sq. triangles
   8 light & 6 dark
4 – sm. half-sq. triangles
   light

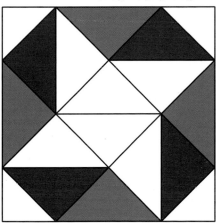

July Fourth

block sizes 6", 8", 10"

14 – lg. quarter-sq. triangles
   6 white, 4 red & 4 blue
4 – sm. half-sq. triangles
   white

never share the previous cut. Always move the template over, so each cut is a fresh one. If you have made an error in cutting, you will only be repeating it across the strip.

STAR PUZZLE

Margrette Carr
San Diego, CA

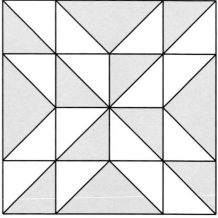

Star Puzzle
Barbara Fritchie Star
Pieced Star
Pierced Star

2 colors

block sizes 6", 8", 10"

- 4 – lg. quarter-sq. triangles
  dark
- 24 – sm. half-sq. triangles
  16 light & 8 dark

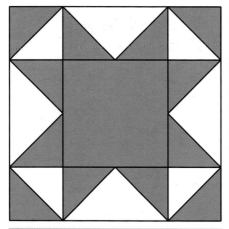

Magic Cross Design

block sizes 6", 8", 10"

- 1 – lg. square, dark
- 4 – lg. quarter-sq. triangles, light
- 16 – sm. half-sq. triangles
  4 light & 12 dark

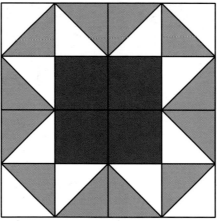

Star Wreath

3 colors

block sizes 6", 8", 10", 12"

- 4 – med. squares, dark
- 24 – med. half-sq. triangles
  12 light & 12 medium

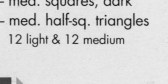

Grandma's Hop-Scotch

3 colors

block sizes 6", 9", 12"

24 – sm. quarter-sq. triangles
  10 light, 6 medium & 8 dark

6 – sm. half-sq. triangles
  2 light, 2 medium & 2 dark

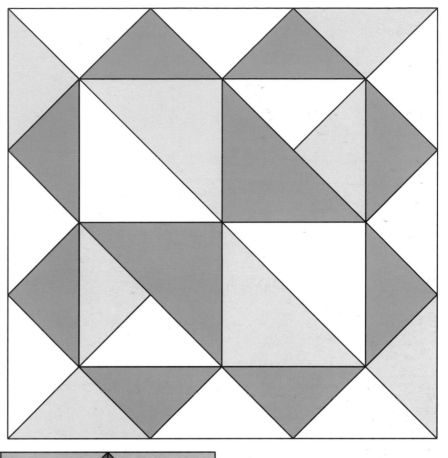

Block of Many Triangles

3 colors

block sizes 6", 8", 12"

28 – med. half-sq. triangles
  2 light, 8 medium & 18 dark

8 – sm. quarter-sq. triangles
  4 light & 4 medium

Pat Yamin ◆ **back** *to* BASICS

Wind Blown Square Variation Whirlpools

block sizes 6", 8", 10"

8 – lg. quarter-sq. triangles
  4 light, 2 medium & 2 dark

16 – sm. half-sq. triangles
  8 light, 4 medium & 4 dark

Mosaic #8

block sizes 6", 8", 10"

4 – lg. quarter-sq. triangles
  dark

24 – sm. half-sq. triangles
  16 light & 8 dark

t his fun block has four sections. The top and bottom portions are duplicates and stacked above each other.

Ozark Mountains Stacked Pyramids
block sizes 6", 8", 10", 12"

20 – med. half-sq. triangles
   4 light, 4 medium
   8 medium-dark & 4 dark
24 – sm. quarter-sq. triangles
   16 light & 8 medium-light

Mosaic #1
block sizes 6", 8", 10"

- 6 – lg. quarter-sq. triangles
  2 medium & 4 dark
- 20 – sm. half-sq. triangles
  16 light & 4 dark

Keep your thimble in your change purse. This way you will always know where it is.

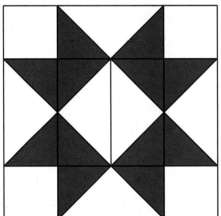

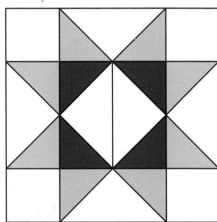

Ribbon Star
2 colors
block sizes 6", 8", 10"

- 6 – lg. quarter-sq. triangles
  light
- 4 – sm. squares, light
- 12 – sm. half-sq. triangles, dark

Variable Star
3 colors
block sizes 6", 8", 10"

- 6 – lg. quarter-sq. triangles
  light
- 4 – sm. squares, light
- 12 – sm. half-sq. triangles
  8 medium & 4 dark

Belle's Favorite

block sizes 6", 8", 10"

8 – sm. squares
    4 light & 4 dark
4 – sm. half-sq. triangles, light
6 – lg. quarter-sq. triangles
    2 light & 4 dark

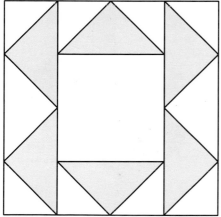

W hen you are buying fabric, buy a yard of the wildest fabric you can find. When you cut it using templates, it will make your quilt sparkle.

Buzzard's Roost

block sizes 6", 8", 10"

1 – lg. square, light
8 – lg. quarter-sq. triangles
    2 light & 6 dark
8 – sm. half-sq. triangles
    light

S ave all those old cotton pillow cases you have to store your finished quilts. Another idea is to buy a vintage pillow case with embroidery and use it to wrap a quilt gift.

Lover's Lane
block sizes 9", 12"

6 – sm. square, light
60 – sm. half-sq. triangles
  32 light & 28 dark

Use long thin straight pins to hold your pieces together and never sew over them! Keep a pincushion nearby as you work and a small magnet to pick up dropped pins from the floor.

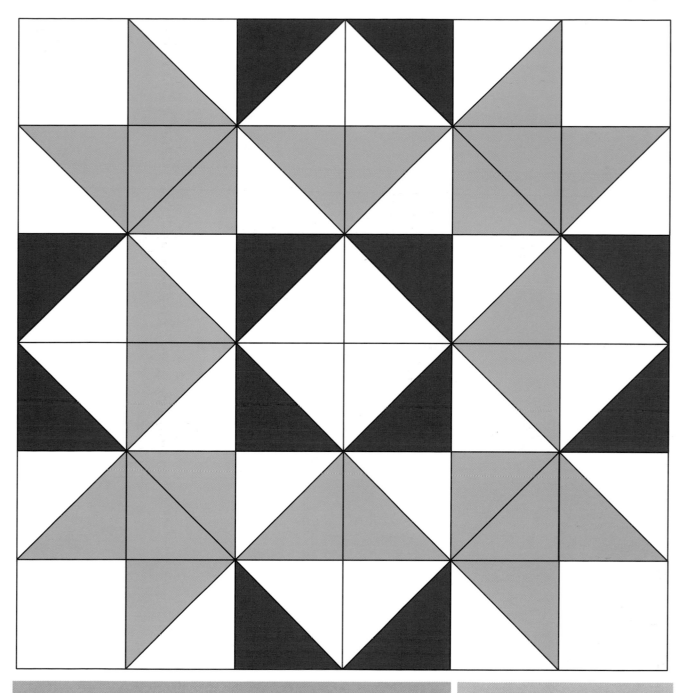

Indian Puzzle

block sizes 6", 9", 12"

4 – sm. squares, light
64 – sm. half-sq. triangles
   28 light, 24 medium &
   12 dark

i f the blocks you try don't work out, make them into pillows and donate them to a local charity. They are also good for practicing your machine quilting stitches.

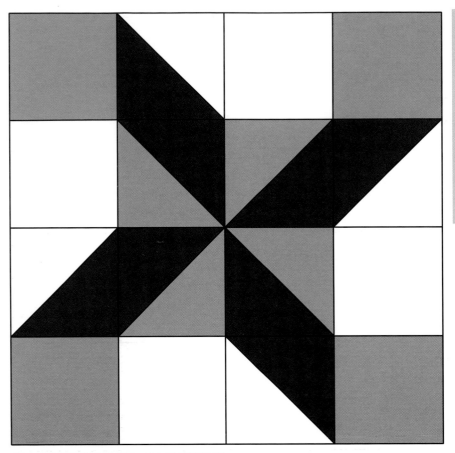

Clay's Choice

block sizes 6", 8", 10", 12"

8 – sm. squares
    4 light & 4 medium
16 – sm. half-sq. triangles
    4 light, 4 medium & 8 dark

 **S**

Butterfly at the Crossroad

block sizes 9", 12"

5 – lg. squares
    4 light & 1 medium
4 – sm. squares, light
8 – sm. half-sq. triangles
    medium
32 – sm. quarter-sq. triangles
    16 light & 16 medium

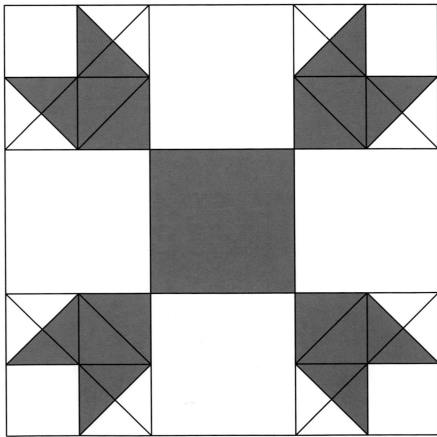

back *to* BASICS ◆ Pat Yamin

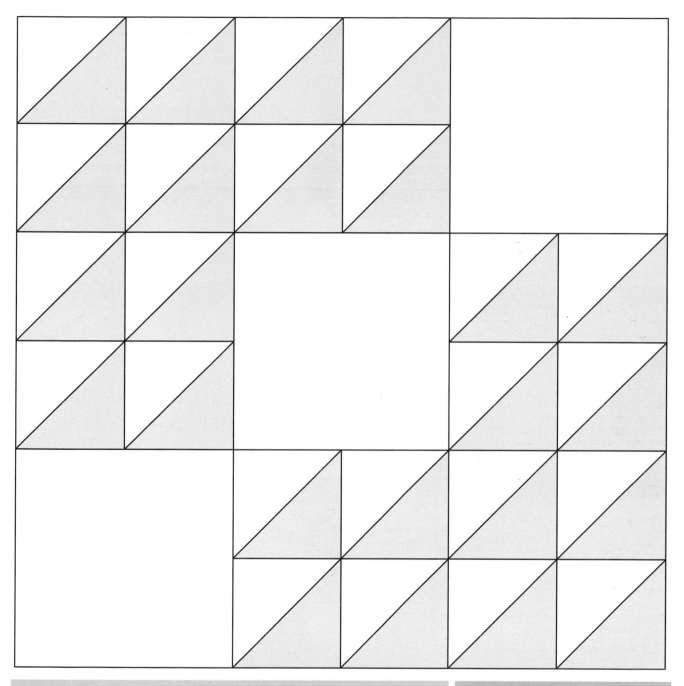

Cut Glass Dish

block sizes 9", 12"

3 – lg. squares, light
48 – sm. half-sq. triangles
24 light & 24 medium

Whenpacking your supplies to take to class, don't forget the presser foot to your machine and extra needles.

Garden Glade

block sizes 6", 8", 12"

4 – med. squares, light
8 – med. half-sq. triangles
    4 light & 4 dark
32 – med. quarter-sq. triangles
    16 light & 16 dark

Clover™ Needlecraft Inc. bias tape maker is the best for making your bias tape. The fabric comes out evenly folded whether cut on the bias or cut on the straight of the grain.

I ook at the block to be sewn. Most blocks are Four-Patches or Nine-Patches. Break down the pieces into units and you will be able to sew straight seams instead of set-in seams.

Windmill Variation

block sizes 6", 8", 12"

5 – lg. half-sq. triangles
    1 light, 1 medium-light & 3 dark
6 – sm. quarter-sq. triangles
    3 light & 3 medium

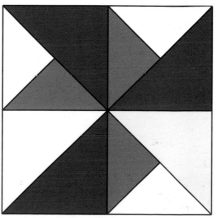

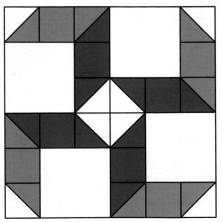

Bachelor's Puzzle
block sizes 6", 12"

4 – lg. squares, light
8 – sm. squares
    4 medium & 4 dark
24 – sm. half-sq. triangles
    8 light, 8 medium & 8 dark

back *to* **BASICS** ◆ Pat Yamin

templates

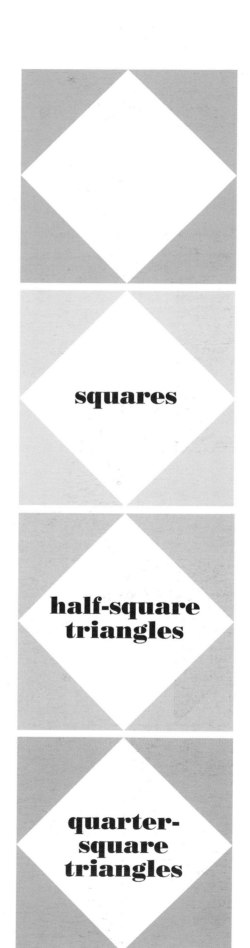

squares

half-square triangles

quarter-square triangles

In patchwork terminology, the word "pattern" is used to identify the design, as well as the physical template used for cutting out the shape in fabric. Paper, cardboard, opaque plastic, or acrylic templates can all be referred to as "templates."

There are two ways for sewing together the pieces you cut out – by machine or by hand. (See the general instructions, pages 14–15.)

To make sturdy templates both techniques require

❖ making extra photocopies of the pages and the sizes you need,

❖ laying the book flat so that the pages are not distorted when copied,

❖ tracing the actual cutting line which already includes the seam allowance,

❖ accurately cutting out the shape(s).

Hand sewers need to use a hole punch to designate the sewing line on the templates (shown as a dot) and then to mark their fabrics accordingly.

Acrylic templates for all 18 pieces are manufactured by Come Quilt with Me, Inc. They are available at local quilt shops, fabric stores, or from your favorite quilting mail order source. (See resources, page 109.)

templates

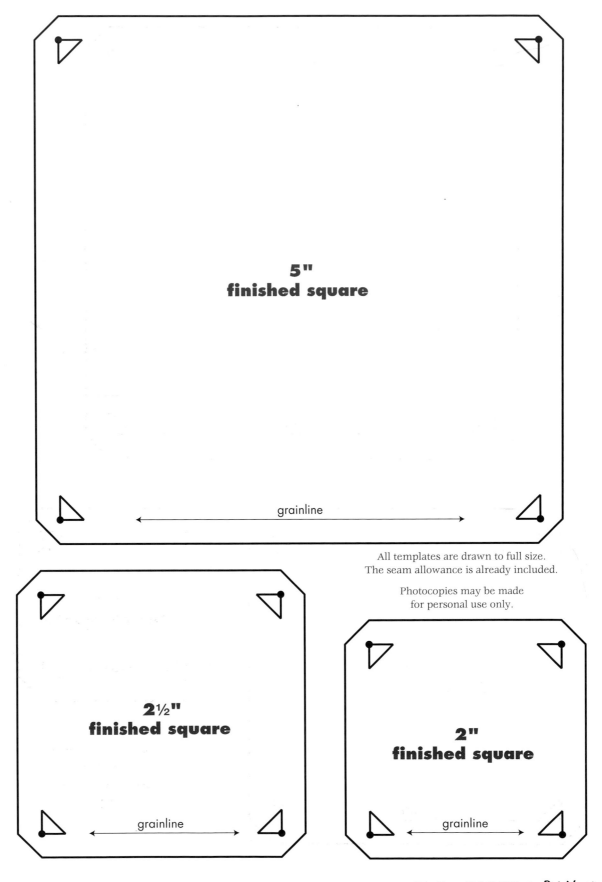

5"
finished square

grainline

All templates are drawn to full size.
The seam allowance is already included.

Photocopies may be made
for personal use only.

2½"
finished square

grainline

2"
finished square

grainline

back *to* BASICS ◆ Pat Yamin

4"
finished square

grainline

3"
finished square

grainline

1½"
finished square

grainline

All templates are drawn to full size.
The seam allowance is already included.

Photocopies may be made
for personal use only.

templates

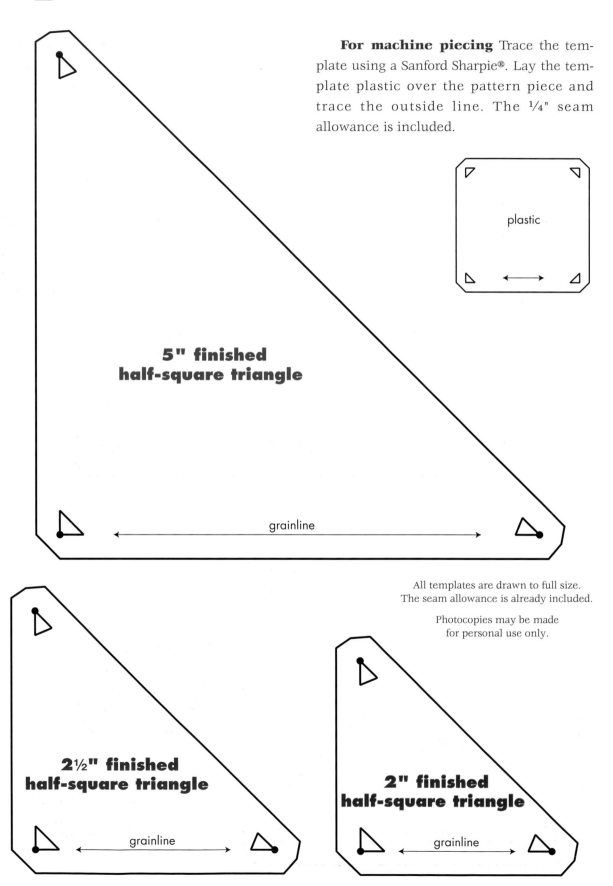

For machine piecing Trace the template using a Sanford Sharpie®. Lay the template plastic over the pattern piece and trace the outside line. The ¼" seam allowance is included.

plastic

5" finished half-square triangle

grainline

All templates are drawn to full size. The seam allowance is already included.

Photocopies may be made for personal use only.

2½" finished half-square triangle

grainline

2" finished half-square triangle

grainline

back *to* BASICS ◆ Pat Yamin

For hand piecing Follow the same method, trace the design, and then use your ⅛" or ¼" hole punch to mark the ¼" at the corners, and maybe once along the seam allowance line.

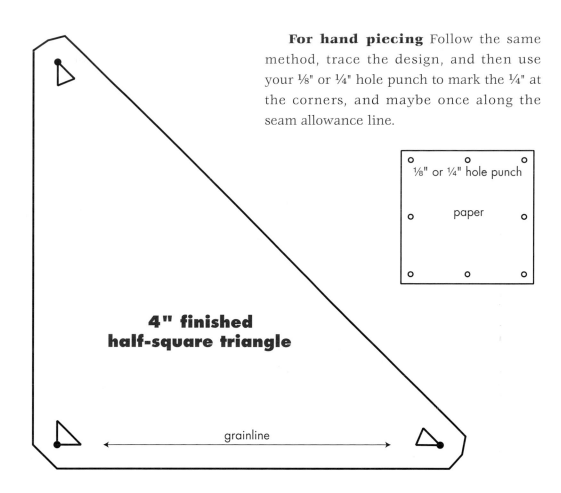

⅛" or ¼" hole punch

paper

4" finished
half-square triangle

grainline

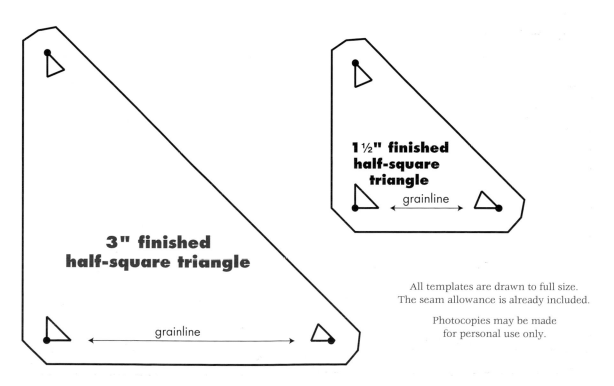

1½" finished
half-square
triangle

grainline

3" finished
half-square triangle

grainline

All templates are drawn to full size.
The seam allowance is already included.

Photocopies may be made
for personal use only.

templates

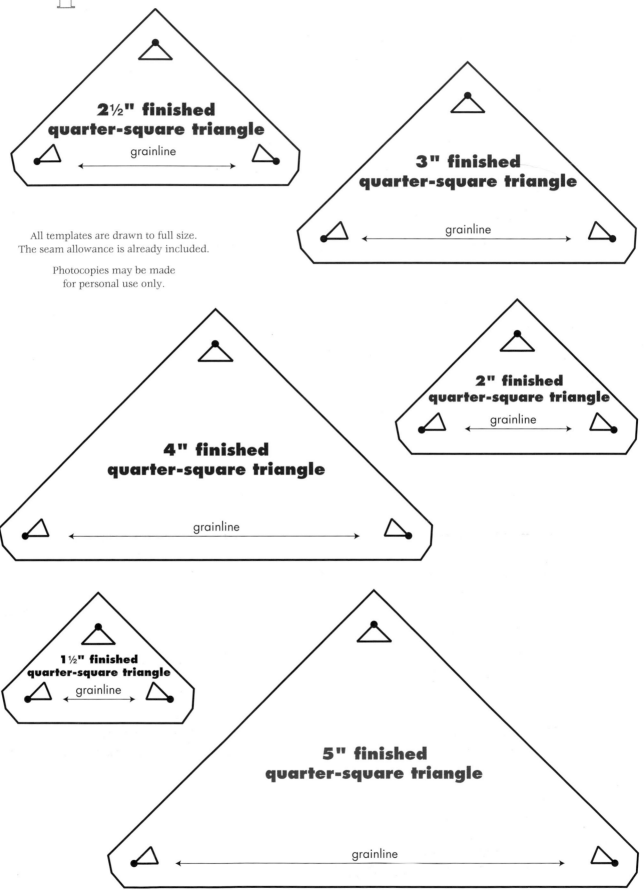

2½" finished quarter-square triangle
grainline

3" finished quarter-square triangle
grainline

All templates are drawn to full size.
The seam allowance is already included.

Photocopies may be made
for personal use only.

4" finished quarter-square triangle
grainline

2" finished quarter-square triangle
grainline

1½" finished quarter-square triangle
grainline

5" finished quarter-square triangle
grainline

back *to* BASICS ◆ Pat Yamin

Brackman, Barbara. *Encyclopedia of Pieced Quilt Patterns.* Paducah, Kentucky: American Quilter's Society, 1993.

Gutcheon, Beth. *The Perfect Patchwork Primer.* New York: Penguin Books, 1973.

Haines, Betty Jo, Charlene Brewer and Carol Combs. *The Ultimate Illustrated Index to the Kansas City Star Quilt Pattern Collection, Volume V.* Oklahoma City, Oklahoma: Central Oklahoma Quilters Guild, Inc., 1990.

Havig, Bettina. *Carrie Hall Blocks: Over 800 Historical Patterns.* Paducah, Kentucky: American Quilter's Society, 1999.

Khin, Yvonne M. *The Collector's Dictionary of Quilt Names & Patterns.* Washington, D.C.: Acropolis Books Ltd., 1980.

Liby, Shirley. *Designing with Nine Patch.* Munice, Indiana: Royal Printing, 1987.

_____. *Exploring Four Patch.* Munice, Indiana: Royal Printing, 1988.

resources

Come Quilt With Me, Inc.
3903 Ave I
Brooklyn, NY 11210
Tel: 718-377-3652
Comequiltwithme@aol.com
Acrylic Templates, Brooklyn Revolver™ cutting mat, Featherweight sewing table.

F. A. Edmunds Co.
6111 S. Sayre
Chicago, IL 60638
Tel: 800-621-1661
www.faersc.com
Quilting hoops and frames

Hearts & Hands
Creative Resource Distributors
826 E. 48th St.
Indianapolis, IN 46205
Exploring Four Patch by Shirley Liby

Hobbs Bonded Fibers
200 S. Commerce Drive
Waco, TX 76710
Tel: 800-433-3357
Hdwilbanks@hobbsbondedfibers.com
Batting

YLI Corporation
161 W. Main Street
Rock Hill, SC 29730
Tel: 803-985-3100
vsmith@ylicorp.com
Quilting thread for hand and machine

Raised in the Midwest, Pat Yamin learned to sew and knit in 4-H clubs. After college, she married and moved to Brooklyn, New York. While pursuing her Master's degree in guidance and counseling, she needed a creative outlet. Pat taught herself to quilt while she became familiar with the city.

Quilting supplies were hard to come by but she learned that Jeff Gutcheon had a studio in SoHo where he sold a few books, batting, and his line of fabric. Pat was working as a vocational counselor to high school seniors and quilting kept her sane in the evenings. She moved from an apartment to a Victorian-style home and began teaching quilting classes in the evenings. Pat's classes became popular, and in no time, she was teaching four nights a week in Manhattan, conducting workshops in her home studio on the weekends, and working full time in counseling.

Pat started a mail-order company called Come Quilt With Me in 1981. She had an inventory of quilting supplies for her students and filled mail orders as well. In 1984 her son Jared was born to her joy and delight. He is now working in the business with her.

In researching the quilting field, Pat decided to design and manufacture acrylic templates. She took the first sets to the Houston Quilt Market in 1991. The company started with traditional patterns and an instruction booklet with each set. Then customers began asking for individual shapes, thus, the A La Carte line was born. The company now carries over 50 patterns.

While designing templates, Pat developed another product. This rotating cutting surface was stable, portable, and economical. After much research into the project, Pat's son came up with the name Brooklyn Revolver™ because of all their connections to Brooklyn. The first Brooklyn Revolver was 9" in diameter. After listening to customers and their needs, a popular 14" size was developed.

Pat teaches at many national shows. She has taught in Houston, both at Quilt Market and Quilt Festival; Vermont Quilt Festival; Pennsylvania Quilt Extravaganza; Pacific International Quilt Festival; World Quilt and Textile Show; Road to California; Williamsburg Quilt Show; Quilter's Gathering; Bernina University; plus many others. She was the quilting consultant for the movie *Sweet Liberty* with Alan Alda. Pat has also appeared on *Quilting with Kaye Wood* and *Quilt Central* with Donna Wilder and Janie Donaldson. She is the author of *Look What I See* (ASN Publishing, 2001) which features her popular hexagon and triangle templates.

Through teaching at over 25 shows a year and her experience with her company, Pat is aware of quilter's needs and desires. She will continue to be present at the shows, meet the people who have helped her along the way, and develop more products to make their lives easier and quilting more fun.

other AQS books

this is only a small selection of the books available from the American Quilter's Society. AQS books are known worldwide for timely topics, clear writing, beautiful color photos, and accurate illustrations and patterns. The following books are available from your local bookseller, quilt shop, or public library.

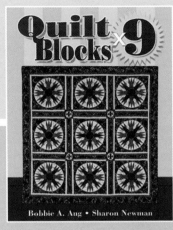

#6298   us$24.95   #6076   us$21.95   #6073   us$19.95

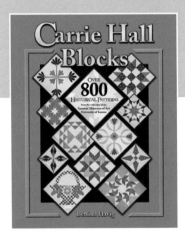

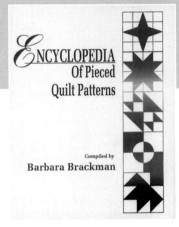

#6212   us$25.95   #4957   us$34.95   #3468   us$34.95

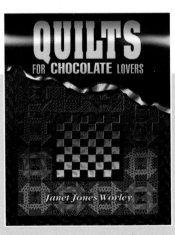

#5844   us$21.95   #5758   us$19.95   #6074   us$21.95